MORAN & PROCTOR

OR & FREEMAN

TOR, FREEMAN & MUESER

WORTH & JOHNSTON

ISTON & DESIMONE

MUESER RUTLEDGE CONSULTING ENGINEERS

75 Years of Foundation Engineering

MUESER RUTLEDGE CONSULTING ENGINEERS
A History of the Firm

By Wilbur Cross, in Collaboration with Partners of the Firm.

BENJAMIN

©1985 by Mueser Rutledge Consulting Engineers.
All rights reserved.

Library of Congress Catalog Number: 85-73198

ISBN: 0-87502-170-0

Produced and published by The Benjamin Company, Inc.
One Westchester Plaza
Elmsford, New York 10523

Printed and bound in the United States of America

First printing: November 1985

CONTENTS

PREFACE: 7

CHAPTER 1: DANIEL E. MORAN: A CONTINUING LEGACY 11

The opening chapter presents a profile of Daniel E. Moran, founder of the firm; recounting his early experiences in foundation engineering and the events leading to the establishment of his own professional practice.

CHAPTER 2: FROM HISTORICAL BEGINNINGS 25

The development of the new firm is discussed with the emphasis on strengthening of the firm with additional partners who helped shape its policies and practice.

CHAPTER 3: BUILDING FOUNDATIONS 35

Shifting from the general to the specific, this chapter focuses on the design and construction of building foundations; highlighting solutions to difficult challenges. The chronological coverage ranges from 1916 to the present with a wide variety of types of buildings.

CHAPTER 4: BRIDGE FOUNDATIONS 55

The firm's early work on bridges and the evolution of patented methods of foundation construction are related, including development of solutions to difficult site conditions.

CHAPTER 5: TUNNELS, SUBWAYS, HIGHWAYS, AIRFIELDS, AND 71
OTHER TRANSPORTATION FACILITIES

This section presents the reader with a cross section of the application of foundation engineering in the many fields of transportation, including tunnels, highways, airports, as well as railroads and subways.

CHAPTER 6: NATIONAL DEFENSE 85

This chapter relates the firm's involvement in World War II jobs such as drydocks and shipbuilding facilities as well as postwar assignments ranging from offshore radar towers to nuclear submarine facilities.

CHAPTER 7: MARINE STRUCTURES AND PORT DEVELOPMENT 99

The examples presented here of docks, offshore moorings, berthing and unloading piers, marine terminals, and other waterfront structures in difficult locations in the U.S. and abroad, demonstrate the special challenges facing the foundation engineer in designing marine facilities.

CHAPTER 8: DAMS, RESERVOIRS, POWER PLANTS, AND WASTE TREATMENT   113

Starting with an example of rehabilitation of a failed dam that had been built in 1894, the text explores the special problems inherent in water related projects.

CHAPTER 9: URBAN AND SITE DEVELOPMENT   127

As shown by examples covered here, the foundation engineer can make substantial contributions on projects which reclaim marginal lands or develop large parcels of new land for a variety of purposes.

CHAPTER 10: INDUSTRIAL DEVELOPMENTS   145

This chapter portrays the firm's involvement over the years in meeting developing needs of major industries including metals, energy, cement, and rubber.

CHAPTER 11: RESEARCH, FIELD INVESTIGATIONS, AND TESTING   155

Daniel E. Moran and others are seen experimenting with soil mechanics and testing long before foundation engineering became "scientific" in its applications. The text also discusses the historical problems of accurate sampling and analysis, and the development of the soil laboratory as we know it today.

CHAPTER 12: CONCLUSION   165

This brief concluding chapter focuses on the World Financial Center at Battery Park City as an example of the multi-faceted problems and challenges that encompass the field of foundation engineering. The organizational philosophies developed by the firm over the years to foster the skills of engineers to handle these challenges are described.

REFERENCES: 168

TABLES: 170

INDEX: 190

LIST OF TABLES

Moran's Patents	170
Partnership History	171
Chronological List of Partners	172
Chronological List of Associates	173
Typical Building Foundation Projects	174
Typical Bridge Foundation Projects	176
Typical Transportation Facility Projects	178
Typical Projects Related to National Defense	180
Typical Marine Structure and Port Development Projects	182
Typical Dam, Reservoir, Power Plant, and Waste Treatment Projects	184
Typical Site Development Projects on Marginal Ground	186
Typical Industrial Projects	188

6

"Foundation design has kept pace with the demands of the superstructure and has utilized new materials and facilities as they became available. If the progress has not been spectacular, it has been sufficient; and we may count with confidence on the engineers of tomorrow to develop the foundation art farther as rapidly as may be required by the new problems which will surely result from progress in other fields." — Daniel E. Moran

Engineering News-Record
April 17, 1924

PREFACE

When the Construction Division of the American Society of Civil Engineers published its "Golden Jubilee" yearbook in 1975, it listed 21 projects that were considered to be "Milestones in Construction History" during the previous 50 years. It is significant that the firm of Mueser Rutledge Consulting Engineers, through its earlier partnerships, was directly involved with more than half of these landmark engineering achievements.

Mention of this participation helps to focus on the fact that foundation and geotechnical engineering is fundamental to most major construction operations. The purpose of this book, published upon the occasion of the firm's 75th anniversary, is to present the firm's involvement in an overview of foundation engineering as it has evolved from a personal skill understood by a small coterie of professionals to an engineering science practiced by an increasing number of specialists.

While the contents of the chapters that follow are focused largely on the work of the firm, they do describe a series of pertinent projects for all who are interested in foundation, geotechnical, structural, and waterfront engineering. We have tried to be objective, both in our approach to the subject and in our discussions of situations, conditions, problems, and solutions. If we have occasionally seemed to dramatize pioneering, creativity, and the development of improved techniques, we do so with a purpose other than enhancing our professional image.

8

The Partners of Mueser Rutledge Consulting Engineers, August 1985. Standing, left to right: Dominic A. Zarrella, Edmund M. Burke, George J. Tamaro. Seated: Warren H. Anderson, Elmer A. Richards, James P. Gould.

Innovation is the lifeblood of engineering, common to all its branches. Discussing the history of our activities in this field is a way to provide the reader with an understanding of the progress, as well as the limitations, in our area of practice.

That is not to say that we shy away from voicing pride in what has been accomplished. The firm's worldwide practice has been established because of our reputation for providing solutions to difficult and often unusual foundation problems. But we are equally desirous of having people acquire a better understanding of what foundation engineering is all about. That is our specialty and we have committed ourselves to the pursuit of excellence within its confines.

It is our mutual hope that this volume will be informative and useful to professional and lay readers alike. It is our story, but it is also the story of many hundreds of other firms with whom we have been associated in ventures, large and small, ranging around the globe.

THE PARTNERS OF MUESER RUTLEDGE
CONSULTING ENGINEERS

Daniel E. Moran, Vice President and Chief Engineer, the Foundation Company, circa 1910

CHAPTER 1
DANIEL E. MORAN: A CONTINUING LEGACY

"Embodying the highest type of engineering skill, the personality and career of Daniel E. Moran brought to his profession more than the inspiration of rare ability . . . He added so greatly to foundation-building practice as to transform what before his time was little more than a random activity into a well-established art."

Engineering-News Record
Obituary July 15, 1937

As an engineer commencing what was to be a long and rewarding career, Daniel E. Moran possessed several unique gifts. One of them was an intense curiosity. He was constantly asking himself why something worked the way it did, and what could be done to make it work better. Had he been a research scientist, this outlook might have been perfectly acceptable to his employer. But as a young, relatively inexperienced engineer on the staff of a New York City contractor, his ingenuous philosophy was constantly getting him into trouble. When he undertook a project, he could not resist questioning the whats, whys, and wherefores of the job.

As will be recounted later in this chapter, it was significant that Moran's first major accomplishment as an engineer would come about because he had undertaken what his employer considered a "waste of time."

His long career as a foundation engineer began when he was employed, early in 1889, by General Charles Sooysmith, one of the great foundation specialists of the nineteenth century. It was an era when engineers spent most of their time in the field and rarely saw the inside of an office. Moran, who had logged five years of rather varied experience as an engineer since his graduation from Columbia University School of Mines in June 1884, was fascinated by the challenge of one of his undertakings. He was assigned by Sooysmith, the contractor, as assistant superintendent and technical observer for construction of a mine shaft at Iron Mountain, Michigan, for the Chapin Mining Company.

The specific problem lay in the fact that the route of the proposed shaft lay directly through a deep running sand formation, which suggested long delays, extra costs, and a certain amount of danger. But Sooysmith had rights to a German patent that was nothing short of ingenious in its day: freezing the loose sand so that it would become solid and stable. Moran worked diligently on this project for several months until the job was completed in the summer of 1889.

It was typical of his curiosity that he noted every detail of the method of driving freeze pipes and circulating a brine refrigerant through them until an annulus of frozen ground, five feet thick, eventually formed around the perimeter of the shaft. He took copious notes, asked innumerable questions, and later wrote a highly professional account for the *School of Mines Quarterly*.

It was not surprising that Moran, with his active curiosity and eye for detail, would sooner or later evaluate some of his firm's methods and procedures to determine whether they could be improved. Sooysmith's principal business was the construction of bridge piers, particularly those sunk through use of pneumatic caissons. Moran used every opportunity to study the designs and methods then in use. His doubts about certain methods were confirmed one day when he was working on the Harlem River Bridge and witnessed an accident. The sudden downward movement of a caisson crushed the lower extension of what was then known as the "O'Conner Bucket." This was the excavation air lock that was in common use. Several lives were lost in this accident, tragically not

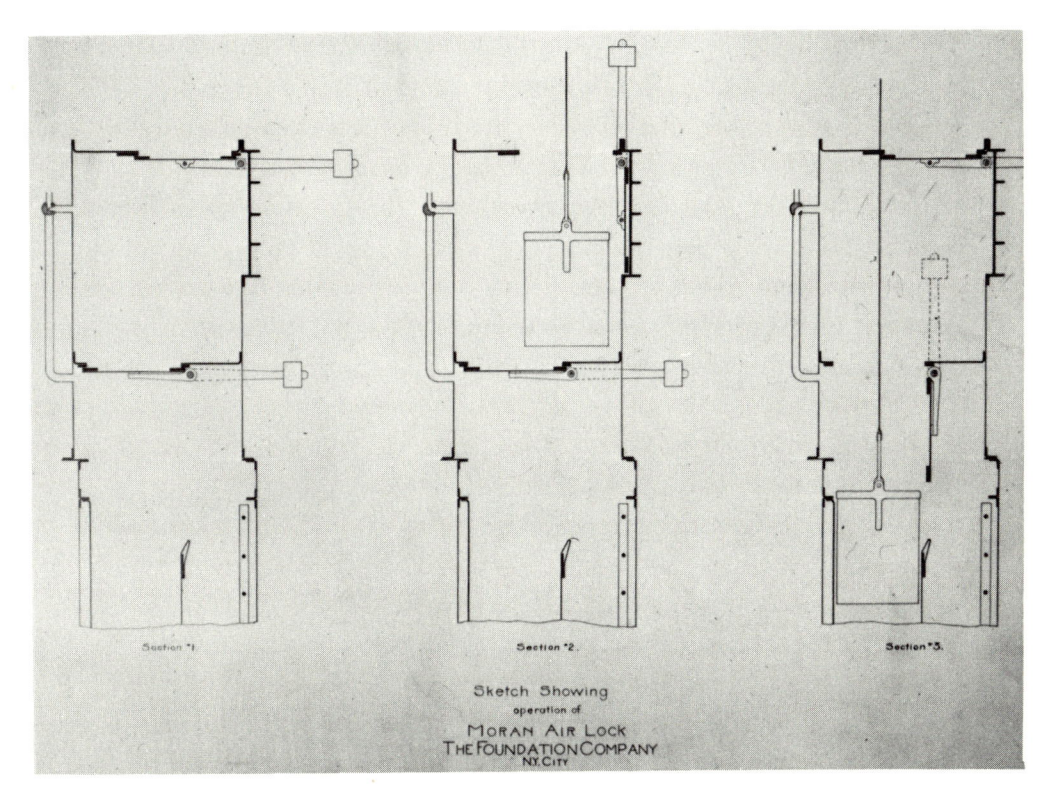

Moran Air Lock. In 1892, eighteen years before founding his own foundation engineering firm, Daniel E. Moran invented improvements in the air lock that greatly facilitated the use of the pneumatic method of pier construction. His device facilitated the removal of materials from beneath the surface and enhanced the safety conditions for work crews laboring at great depths below the water surface.

the first and certainly not the last unless the old style of air locks were improved and made safer.

"I looked up all the data we had on the subject and started to design a safe and economical lock," recalled Moran.[1] Sooysmith, annoyed by the young engineer's brashness in assuming that he could make such improvements, ordered him not to waste the firm's time, or his own. Undaunted, Moran continued his studies on his own time and soon had devised an air lock that satisfied his own rigid requirements. He then patented* it, convinced Sooysmith that it would work, and arranged to have one built for the firm, free of royalty, in 1892. The lock was of the top-and-bottom-door type. The top was constructed with two hinged doors that met at the center, where the hoist rope passed through a stuffing box that retained the desired air pressure during operations. Moran's invention was designed to enhance the speed and economy of pneumatic caisson work, making it possible to lower empty buckets through the lock and down the shaft directly to the floor of the working chambers and to hoist the loaded buckets without extra maneuvering or delay.

The lock proved itself a short time later, and in quite a dramatic manner. In 1892, Moran was to help design the caissons for the McCombs Dam Bridge, crossing the Harlem River at 155th Street in New York City. Although he had already built one of his own locks, it was not being used on this particular job. While work was in progress, both bucket locks on the job — the old, conventional type — failed before the large caisson was sunk to its final depth. One became hopelessly jammed at the bottom of the shaft. The new Moran lock, which had been stored near the site, was brought out and secured to the top of the shaft. The old buckets were removed through it and the work proceeded without further mishap.

So efficient was the basic design of the Moran air lock that it was still in use, with certain modifications and improvements, at the time of Moran's death in 1937. In 1903, Moran also invented and patented a pneumatic caisson that had a reinforced concrete working chamber integral with the caisson body.

"To a certain extent," said *Engineering News-Record* almost a quarter of a century after Moran's obituary, "it was this type of caisson that made possible the New York skyscrapers in lower Manhattan and permitted bridge foundations to be carried to theretofore unattainable depths."[2]

* For a list of Moran's patents, see page 170.

The Foundation Company

By the end of the nineteenth century, Daniel E. Moran had determined his concept of what was to be a long and satisfying career. For him, the great engineering challenge lay in foundations. In studying the great cities of the world, ever curious to determine what motivated their locations and planning, he discovered a significant, and contradictory, factor that seemed to be common to most of these historic metropolises.

"The commerce of nations," he was to write later in an article in *Harper's Weekly,* "developing along the lines of least resistance, blazes its trail along the waterways of every country. Where land and water traffic meet, where ocean steamers exchange with inland lines of transportation, there commerce makes its exchanges, reshipments, purchases, and sales, and there it demands wharves and warehouses, banks and offices — and there are developed the great cities of the world."

The contradiction came in the fact that, as he defined it, "The conjunction of land and water, however favorable to the development of a great city, bodes trouble for the builder seeking suitable foundation. The alluvial deposits found near the mouths of rivers, the fine sands of beaches, and the mud banks of bays and harbors are not suitable materials on which to impose great weights."[3]

As he studied the major cities of the world, he saw that one after the other faced just such massive problems: Boston, Detroit, Cleveland, and Chicago were built on deep beds of late Pleistocene clay; the north German and Dutch ports, as well as Cairo and New Orleans, were located on recent delta formations; the site of St. Petersburg was a marsh; and Mexico City was literally floating on a thin crust under which lay an almost bottomless lake of mud. As for New York City, it had a backbone of solid rock, but a southern portion of Manhattan, where much of the new construction was under way and planned, was covered by recent glacial sediments. And just across the Hudson River, in New

Jersey, the waterfront areas occupied by numerous terminals and other freight-handling facilities were "little better than banks of oozy mud."

With these facts in mind, and well aware that there had been few advances in deep foundation methods and operations since the Civil War or earlier, Moran decided that he would devote his major efforts to this field of engineering. It was a natural step for him when, in 1901, he formed the Foundation Company with two other partners, Franklin Remington and Edwin S. Jarrett. The company started with borrowed capital of $25,000. It speaks well for the professional skills and the intuition of the founders that the company was soon referred to as "the leading builder of deep and difficult foundations in the United States."[4]

He was to continue with the Foundation Company for almost ten years, before resigning to start a new firm. Yet he continued as a specialist in this field, recognized as a leading authority right up to the time of his death in 1937. He was to become known unofficially as the "Dean of American Foundation Experts." The title was an appropriate one, for he brought to his profession a scholarly insight and dedication to research that resulted in practical achievements. He deplored the fact that, while technologists had accomplished so much in the fields of communication, transportation, and surface construction, they were ignorant when it came to subsurface engineering.

Moran often used colorful and graphic descriptions to dramatize the weaknesses in his selected field. He made the point that even inexperienced engineering students were very familiar with the materials, stresses, and designs of the *aboveground* portions of a building, yet neither they nor more experienced engineers were clear about these elements when they went below the footing. In one instance, he likened the engineers to spectators watching a flimsy vessel embark on a voyage of discovery to the unknown: ". . . at the level of the footing, where the resultants of all the forces which act on the structure pass from well-ordered and narrow paths into the unknown, into the freedom of indeterminate stresses, there the engineer stands, waving the forces good-bye, and wishing them a safe voyage into a safe harbor."[5]

Powers of Observation as a Motivating Force

"Daniel E. Moran was phenomenally keen of observation," reported a column in *Engineering News of the Week* that typified many of the assessments of him during his professional lifetime, "and as a result had a more thorough intuitive knowledge of soils and their behavior than anyone in his generation."[6]

It is easy to analyze the reasons for this perceptiveness. Moran himself liked to oversimplify the key to his long record of achievement, frequently saying, "I *should* know what I'm doing, since I've been privileged to look into more holes in the ground than most men, and have learned something of value from each one."[7] What he saw, however, was insignificant compared with what he *did*. He and his partners had barely completed the structuring of the Foundation Company when he began experimenting with wide varieties of soils. He meticulously observed the results and recorded data on the progressive settlement of fine-grained materials under load. He concluded that the volumetric consolidation became equal to the volume of water that was expelled from a loaded soil — a conclusion that was far in advance of the limited technology of his day.

Moran found many contradictions and challenges in the field of his choice. Rather than frustrating and aggravating him, however, they served to pique his unquenchable curiosity and motivate him to seek solutions to continuing problems. The only enigma that seemed to test his patience was one of semantics. He regularly deplored the lack of practical definitions for the overburden that covered rock strata. "We have no common word in the English language," he said, "covering this collection of various materials; nor in the engineering profession, any technical word . . . the best definition I know of is 'material — other than rock.' That is a stupid way to define it, but the engineer has not yet, in his vocabulary, a better word."[8]

He constantly sought ways of establishing a clearer and more understandable professional interpretation of the term "foundation." It might mean a variety of things, he said, sometimes referring to the structure and sometimes to the natural strata upon which the structure rested. It could include almost any substance, from masses of solid bedrock to boulders, torrential sediments, or plastic clay. As he discovered when advising clients involved in contract disputes, the word *foundation* in a contract or insurance policy was often meaningless. There was no distinct line that could be drawn, by owner, insurance broker, contractor, or engineer as to what was legally the foundation and what was not.

Although Moran was among the first to understand the nature of soils as they applied to engineering (and particularly the significance of volumetric changes in clay and silt under loads), he was cautious about defining his work as "scientific." Even many years later, with hundreds of experiments behind him, he expressed the conviction that "foundation engineering is an art for which there is no substitute for judgement based on wide experience," and that this art must be treated "only as a valuable tool to be used by the experienced foundation engineer, never as a means unto itself."

From 1901 until 1910, at the Foundation Company in New York City, Moran designed and helped to construct many deep and difficult foundations for skyscrapers, bridges, dams, power plants, and mine shafts throughout the country. So many of these were in Manhattan, including such structures as the Trinity, Woolworth, Whitehall, Singer, Banker's Trust, and Municipal buildings, that he became popularly known as "the man who made the skyline of New York."[9]

He was instrumental in some of the most notable foundation developments of that era, including working chambers that were entirely made of concrete; interior braces and exterior forms that could be removed when the job was completed, vastly increasing space of improved quality in basements and subbasements; the improvement and installation of cast-in-place reinforced-concrete piles, interlocking steel sheet piling, and cement waterproofing; and methods for excavating deep caissons in unstable soils.

The Woolworth Building before its completion in 1913, when it became famous as the tallest building in the world. Pneumatic caissons were installed for the foundation by the Foundation Company, founded by Dan Moran and two partners in 1901.

Birth of a New Company

In 1910, Daniel Moran felt that he could contribute more to the knowledge of foundation engineering and enhance his own career by forming a new company as a consultant in the field of substructures. He resigned from the Foundation Company and on May 1 of that year began doing business under his own name at 55 Liberty Street in New York City. He continued, as before, to spend a great deal of time investigating soils and experimenting with new methods of designing foundations to overcome the problems of existing subsurface conditions or take advantage of the positive factors of the specific sites.

In 1909, the year before he left the Foundation Company to form his own engineering firm, Daniel E. Moran (left) attended the laying of the cornerstone of the Municipal Building in lower Manhattan. Mayor George B. McClellan (in top hat) presided. This was one of the first of many substructures Moran would complete for public and government buildings of many types.

Moran worked as an individual consultant until, two years later, he was joined by Charles F. Maurice, a former associate at the Foundation Company. But the firm did not really begin to expand until the end of the decade, when Carlton S. Proctor joined what was thereafter to become a new partnership, Moran, Maurice & Proctor. All three principals — as was to be the case throughout the history of the firm — were committed by choice to foundation engineering and had no intention of expanding into other fields of engineering.

As a consultant during that first decade and into the mid-twenties, Moran designed and supervised foundation work for many buildings in New York City, such as the Cunard Building, American Telephone and Telegraph Building, the New York Stock Exchange, the New York County Court House, the Federal Reserve Bank, the Barclay-Vesey Telephone Building, the J.P. Morgan Building, and the Bank of America. Outside of New York, the firm worked on the Travelers Insurance Company Building in Hartford, Harkness Memorial Tower at Yale, the Washington Monument and the National Academy of Science, and the Ohio Bell Telephone Company Building in Cleveland.

The list of bridges included the Philadelphia-Camden Bridge, Mid-Hudson Bridge at Poughkeepsie, and the East 16th Street Bridge in Pittsburgh. Dams and powerhouses were constructed at Allison and Wilkes-Barre, Pennsylvania; Ducktown, Tennessee; Glens Falls, New York; Galveston, Texas; New London, Connecticut; and Saskatoon, Canada. These were followed in the 1930s by such notable works as the San Francisco-Oakland Bay, Golden Gate, and Tacoma Narrows bridges.

Many of these projects called for new techniques and varying approaches to foundation engineering. This was exactly the kind of challenge on which Daniel Moran thrived. It was his professional policy and personal habit to question the traditional ways of doing things, in a direct and forthright manner. In pursuing this strategy, he spared no one — including himself. His readiness to break with precedent was well demonstrated. Although he had become a recognized leader in pneumatic foundation methods, he later consistently opposed their use until all other construction procedures had been studied and evaluated for

Carlton S. Proctor had been a professional engineer for 43 years at the time he retired from the firm (then Moran, Proctor, Mueser & Rutledge) in 1960. He served as a consultant for bridges, dams, power stations, tunnels, navigation docks, skyscrapers, and many other structures, and was a past president of the American Society of Civil Engineers and The Moles.

Charles F. Maurice devoted his entire professional life to foundation engineering, mainly in lower Manhattan, where he served as consultant for notable structures like the New York Stock Exchange Building. He worked with Daniel Moran at the Foundation Company and joined him shortly after Moran founded his new firm in 1910.

the job. He knew that in many instances he could use alternatives, such as cofferdams for deep building foundations or open dredging for difficult bridge piers, at lower cost.

The First National Bank Building and the City Bank Farmer's Trust Company in New York City would have required pneumatic caissons had they been built before World War I. But when Moran negotiated the contracts to do the foundations, he elected to use open excavations, thus effecting great savings without compromising in any way the major specifications for each job. Paradoxically, he actually pioneered in eliminating some of the very methods he had spent so much effort developing. It was all part of his policy to improve procedures — and then improve upon the improvements!

"Originality and inventiveness were marked traits of Mr. Moran's personality," wrote an engineering editor who had known him well. "He was ever seeking out new paths in the solution of engineering problems, and rarely was content to follow the methods of precedent ... He was a creative genius with a penetrating observation of every soil and foundation condition."[10] This inventiveness is solidly attested to by his numerous patents for building piers, shafts, caissons; subaqueous structures; sand drains; sinking foundations; the storage of gasoline; and of course, the earlier-mentioned air locks.

Moran's genius also lay in the fact that he was what we now designate a "team player." He was little concerned about credit for his inventiveness or his innovations. He was, however, always insistent that his firm, and anyone involved in a particular job, adhere to the policies and attitudes that he had so carefully nurtured. That is one reason the heritage he left his firm when he died, and which has been preserved to the present, reflects the unique qualities that Moran himself brought to the art of foundation engineering. It is one of the reasons, too, that the firm, through 75 years of development, has continued to focus on *foundation* engineering, restricting its field of specialization.

The legacy of Daniel E. Moran, which followed his death on July 3, 1937, at the age of 73, has been one of the most valuable and durable assets of the firm he founded 75 years ago.

The completion of the Benjamin Franklin Bridge between Philadelphia and Camden marked the realization of a century-old plan for connecting the two cities. Daniel Moran, seated at the left in the bucket with Ralph Modjeski and George Webster, represented his firm during an inspection of the caissons while the bridge was under construction.

CHAPTER 2

FROM HISTORICAL BEGINNINGS

"The great bulk of the firm's practice relates to foundations of buildings, bridges, and marine structures . . . Broadly speaking, however, most of the foundation work is of the difficult and specialized variety, so that it has to go farther than the usual consulting engineer firm in working out complete construction procedures."

Engineering-News Record
"Fifty Years in Foundations"

By the beginning of World War I, the young engineering firm was involved with an increasing number of jobs, especially in the metropolitan New York region. There was considerable variety in the work, ranging from lower Manhattan skyscrapers to public buildings, tunnels, bridges, dams, power facilities, churches, banks, and industrial properties. It was significant, though, that Moran's earlier pattern of jobs was not changing and that the new firm in its turn was becoming known for its specialized work in foundations.

Charles F. Maurice was making a name for himself as Moran's partner, though his name was not yet incorporated in the firm's title. Maurice had worked closely with Moran at the Foundation Company several years before and rejoined him in 1912 when Moran's work load became too heavy for a single manager to administer effectively.

The firm began a major job just before the United States entered World War I when it obtained a design contract on the New York City County Court House, which presented a number of unique foundation problems. After interruptions on this and other jobs because of wartime restrictions, the firm resumed normal operations. Shortly after the war, Moran decided to enlarge and reorganize the business. In 1920, the firm became known as Moran, Maurice & Proctor, recognizing Charles Maurice for his eight years of service and adding a new partner, Carlton Proctor.

Proctor, a graduate of Princeton and later honored with the University's Doctorate of Engineering degree, had been a field superintendent in Washington and had served two years as a construction officer with the United States Army prior to joining the firm in September 1919. During World War I, he attained the rank of captain in the Corps of Engineers. Later he was to become president of the Moles in 1949 and president of the American Society of Civil Engineers during its Centennial Year, 1952.

One of the newly reorganized firm's major jobs at the start of the 1920s was the Benjamin Franklin Bridge over the Delaware River between Philadelphia and Camden, which required deep caissons. Moran served as foundation consultant to the advisory board, chaired by Ralph Modjeski. The success of this work led to a number of other bridge projects, including the Mid-Hudson suspension bridge at Poughkeepsie, New York, in 1924 and the combined railway and highway bridge at Vicksburg, Mississippi, a few years later.

By the end of the 1920s, having moved from its downtown location to new offices in mid-Manhattan, the firm was acting as consultants for the foundations of a number of important buildings in widely scattered locations in the U.S. These included, for example, the Toledo Main Telephone Building and the Dayton Main Telephone Building for the Ohio Bell Telephone Company; the Battery Tower in New York City; the Aldred Building in Montreal; the Lefcourt-Newark Building in Newark, New Jersey; and the First National Bank Building in Atlanta.

In 1923, the engineering ranks were strengthened by the arrival of a man who was to make a prominent mark in the field. He was William H. Mueser, a native New Yorker who had obtained a civil engineering degree from the Massachusetts Institute of Technology in 1922 and had just completed a year of graduate studies at the Technische Hochschule in

Carlton S. Proctor (left) presided at The Moles 1950 Awards Dinner and presented then General Dwight D. Eisenhower (second from right) with honorary membership and President Herbert C. Hoover (second from left) with the Association's non-member award. Also shown is Richard E. Dougherty (right) who received the member award.

George L. Freeman gained many years of experience in heavy construction before he joined the firm in 1929, after serving as a vice president of Moran's old firm, the Foundation Company. He was made a partner in 1936 and served for fifteen more years until his retirement.

William H. Mueser joined the firm after graduation from M.I.T. in 1922 and a year of graduate study at the Berlin Technische Hochshule. A dynamic individual, he was recognized as one of the leaders in the field of foundation engineering. He was also a recipient of honors and awards from several engineering societies.

The Bank of Manhattan Building resembled a concrete, steel, and wood puzzle when this photograph was taken in 1929. The installation of foundation columns occurred at the same time as the former buildings on the site were being demolished. This procedure enabled the builder to complete the 71-story structure within one year.

Berlin. He would spend his entire career with the firm and be honored in 1975 in the ASCE's "Golden Jubilee" history as one of the "Top Ten Construction Men" of the previous 50 years. He became known as a "construction man's engineer, always ready to roll up his sleeves and go to work on a knotty problem . . . "[1]

Three years after the untimely death of Charles Maurice in 1926 at the age of 53, the firm's name was changed to Moran & Proctor. That year — 1929 — George L. Freeman joined the team. He had been vice president and chief engineer at the Foundation Company and had specialized in bridge foundations. He would later become known for his work on the Whitestone Bridge in New York, which required one of the deepest caissons ever sunk for a bridge foundation at that time. Seven years after joining, he would also become a partner.

Work in Progress

The middle of the 1920s saw the firm involved with many significant — often innovative — developments in foundation construction in lower Manhattan. One prime example was the Barclay-Vesey Telephone Building. The firm was commissioned to design and supervise the foundation construction, including five basement levels, the deepest of which was more than 70 feet below grade.

Notable examples of the firm's foundation work in the twenties were the Equitable Trust Building in New York's Wall Street district, which won the 1928 Merit Award from *Building Investment* magazine as the "Outstanding Construction Achievement of the Year"; the 23-story Royal Bank Building in Montreal, a monumental structure that encountered serious problems because of the presence on the site of highly pervious glacial outwash below river level; and the 71-story Bank of Manhattan Building, whose foundations had to be built simultaneously with the razing of six old buildings that had covered the site. The firm's resident engineers remained constantly on site during completion of all major projects, giving the firm a reputation for working closely with the builders during all phases of foundation planning and construction.

While this type of work was progressing in the familiar New York setting, the firm was also deeply committed to projects much farther afield. They consisted not only of buildings, but also dams, power facilities, bridges, and highways, among others. One far-flung project was a commission from the Russian government to investigate the feasibility of erecting a great hydroelectric dam on the Svir River, 175 miles northeast of Leningrad. Carlton Proctor made six trips to Russia to inspect the progress of construction.

Another interesting commission in Russia, at the beginning of the 1930s, was a design for foundations of the immense Palace of the Soviets in Moscow. Although never completed, the huge circular building was designed in such a way that it would not be subjected to serious differential settlements under the two circles of columns that were to support and enhance a hemispherical dome. These projects — and others all over the world — took members of the firm to Europe, the Orient, and much of Latin America.

The Palace of the Soviets in Moscow posed special foundation problems when the firm was called in as consultants in 1935. Not only was the site a difficult one, but the building was of unprecedented design: two circles of columns with a heavy dome springing from the inner circle. The Palace was dismantled by the Russians before completion, its steel girders needed for more vital projects during World War II.

Evolving Policies

The geographical scope of operations and the varied nature of the client list suggest that the firm was diversifying and establishing new policies and methods of procedure. Yet such was not the case. It had already demonstrated that success could be achieved by restricting activities to the essential field of foundations and by keeping the firm small enough so that the partners could spend substantial time in the field, exercising engineering control of their projects, rather than having to engage heavily in office administration. It was also determined that the quality of the work could best be assured by maintaining a single design office.

These were some of the factors that shaped the policies and procedures of the firm during the 1920s and into the 1930s and 1940s, continuing to the present. Each partner contributed to the enhancement of these policies so that the leadership continued in an unbroken pattern, despite changes in the firm name and the details of current projects.

In 1939, two years after he became a partner, William Mueser was recognized for his increasing role when the name of the firm was changed to Moran, Proctor, Freeman & Mueser. A number of important projects were completed during the mid to late 1930s, including foundations for the San Francisco-Oakland Bay Bridge, Golden Gate Bridge, and Huey P. Long Bridge over the Mississippi at New Orleans; site development and many of the building foundations for the 1939 New York World's Fair; harbor and port facilities, like the Sparrows Point, Baltimore, ore dock and a floating dry dock for the United States Navy; and the development of Idlewild (now JFK), La Guardia, and other major airports.

Two engineers who were active during this era and who were later to become partners were Robert C. Johnston and Paul Wentworth, who joined the firm in 1935 and 1940, respectively. Johnston was to devote much of his time to deep foundations, marine projects, and site development. Wentworth had been with the Foundation Company, for which he had redesigned earthquake-damaged school buildings in Chile in 1929, and during the 1930s had worked for the Civilian Conservation Corps and for Gibbs and Hill on a Pennsylvania Railroad electrification project. Johnston, like Mueser, spent his entire active career with the firm, except for a period of service during World War II as a Navy Civil Engineer Corps officer when he saw action in the D-Day landings in Normandy and through the advance of the Allies into Germany. He remains a consultant to the firm to this time.

Philip C. Rutledge, who joined the firm in 1952, brought an extensive academic background as well as a logical approach to the firm's practice in the field of foundation engineering. During World War II, he had received a War Department award for developing landing strips for heavy aircraft. (top left)

George T. Gilman, who first joined the firm (then Moran, Maurice, & Proctor) in 1927, served during World War II with Dry Dock Engineers on the design of dry dock facilities for the U.S. Navy Bureau of Yards and Docks. A specialist in foundation work for bridges and skyscrapers, he was the author of various papers on these subjects. (center left)

Salvatore V. DeSimone, who first joined the firm in 1948 and was named a partner in 1966, directed the firm's work on many large projects prior to his early retirement because of ill health. Active on engineering committees, he served in a leadership role for a number of professional organizations and was president of The Moles. (bottom left)

In 1964, the firm became known as Mueser, Rutledge, Wentworth & Johnston. Looking over foundation plans in the conference room at 415 Madison Avenue in the midsixties are (left to right) *Paul M. Wentworth, Philip C. Rutledge, William H. Mueser, and Robert C. Johnston.*

During the war years, the firm was particularly active in national defense projects in the design and construction of dry docks for the Navy. In 1944, after four years with the Dry Dock Engineers, a joint venture of the firm with Frederic R. Harris, Inc.; Parsons, Klapp, Brinckerhoff, & Douglas; and Fay, Spofford & Thorndike, George T. Gilman became a partner. Gilman had been with the firm since 1928. He was only 48 when he died in 1948 after a long illness.

In 1952, following the retirement of George L. Freeman from active service, Philip C. Rutledge joined the firm, bringing with him a wide range of geotechnical experience. He had been chairman of the Department of Civil Engineering at Northwestern University for nine years, formerly professor of civil engineering at Purdue for six years, and earlier had taught at both MIT and Harvard. During World War II, he had served on the Board of Consultants on Airfield Pavements for the Office of the Army Chief of Engineers and had helped to develop landing strips for heavy aircraft. For this work, he was awarded a War Department Certificate of Appreciation. For Waterways Experiment Station, Rutledge had carried out a fundamental research project relating shear strength of clays to their degree of consolidation.

In 1952, the firm became Moran, Proctor, Mueser & Rutledge and continued under this name until 1963 when, for the first time, *two* names were dropped from the title and two added. The firm bore the name Mueser, Rutledge, Wentworth & Johnston from 1963 until 1978. At that time, it was changed to Mueser, Rutledge, Johnston & DeSimone to reflect the retirement of Paul Wentworth in 1977, when he continued as a consultant, and the recognition of Salvatore V. DeSimone as a principal. Although Rutledge and Mueser also retired, in 1977 and 1978, respectively, their names were retained in the title of the firm.

During the firm's 75th Anniversary Year, it was decided to change the name one last time to Mueser Rutledge Consulting Engineers. This decision, while recognizing the names of the senior partners of recent years, will add a sense of continuity to the next quarter-century of operations.

34

Moving an eight-story telephone building without disrupting service was the special challenge faced by the firm when it undertook the project in Indianapolis for the Bell Telephone Company of Indiana. The sequence shows the building (top left) in its original position on the site, (top right) moved to the other side of the lot, (bottom left) being rotated toward final position, and (bottom right) in its new location. Note the rails with radial guidelines on which the 11,000-ton building was moved, the spliced-out telephone cables, and the temporary entranceway, which shifted as the building rotated on its axis.

CHAPTER 3

BUILDING FOUNDATIONS

"Moran and Proctor specialize in foundation work and have been identified with large construction undertakings in many parts of this country and abroad. Owing to the nature of their work, they are frequently in contact with difficult and unusual situations and are often called in on jobs after difficulties have been encountered."

Indiana Telephone News
December 1930

Nothing quite like it had ever been attempted.

Could an eight-story telephone office building weighing 11,000 tons be moved and rotated 90 degrees without in any way disrupting local, long-distance, and house phone services? The Indiana Bell Telephone Company had considered the idea many times in the late 1920s, but had always found the challenges imposing. The building, then the company's main office, was situated on a lot 200 feet square in the heart of Indianapolis. Indiana Bell had planned a new structure on the lot which, when connected to the existing office, would provide facilities for planned expansion for many years.

The problem was that the existing building was in the wrong location, occupying the center of the lot and facing in the wrong direction. Moving and rotating it were not the only challenges. The job would have to be completed quickly, maintaining normal telephone and international telegraph services during the move by regular shifts of 1,000 employees who were on duty, day and night, seven days a week. Building services, such as water, gas, steam, sewerage, and elevators, also had to function normally.

In 1929, with pressure mounting to modernize and broaden its facilities, Indiana Bell made the decision to proceed with the relocation, difficult though it might be. The job clearly required a coordinated team of specialists. Moran & Proctor was retained to investigate the feasibility of the plan, as well as to design the foundations and structural features.

Faced with the challenge, Moran & Proctor pored over its solutions for earlier building foundations. None of them, of course, was the same. However, there were parallel questions and enigmas. Dozens of techniques were considered and rejected, yet with each step leading closer to specific solutions. Moran, Proctor, and the young MIT graduate, William Mueser, comprised the team, all aware that they had to coordinate their work with the engineering department of Indiana Bell, architects, structural engineers, general contractor, and a multitude of technicians and specialists who would be responsible for maintaining services and internal operations at all times.

The solution to the problem was unprecedented for a building of the size and weight of Bell's headquarters. Yet everything worked smoothly and according to plan. Basically, it was a three-part operation: (1) paving the area with a level, one-foot-thick concrete mat covered by a timber cushion carrying hundreds of steel rails; (2) riveting jacking brackets to the building columns and raising the structure by means of powerful screw jacks; and (3) transferring the column loads to rollers and moving the building in the desired direction with the screw jacks, aided by steam-powered block-and-tackle units. The building was first moved in a southerly direction for 52 feet, after which the shoes and rollers were reset, and then turned about a pivot point. The force needed to move the structure was in the range of ten to twelve percent of the building weight.

The engineering design was so finely tuned that it was necessary to raise each column less than one-quarter of an inch to transfer the load to the rollers. Even more significant, the building never deviated more than two inches horizontally from its intended course during the seventeen days required to move it to its new location. During this entire period, telephone exchanges continued to function as usual, operating through cable extensions that were flexible enough to rotate with the building. Gas, water, sewer, and steam-heat lines were maintained through bypass valves; and the central elevator continued in operation. The entire transition was so slow that employees at work sensed no movement at all.

While the Indiana Bell project was not the largest of the firm's jobs during this era, it was certainly unique. As the chief engineer of the Indiana Bell Telephone Company reported later, "The building has been moved as planned, placed on the exact spot indicated, within the time schedules, within the cost estimates, without interruption to service, and without mishap."[1]

The Barclay-Vesey Telephone Building imposed several unprecedented requirements for foundation construction when it was built in the 1920s. Planned for a location in lower Manhattan that had at one time been outside of the original shoreline of the Hudson River, the substructure required a continuous concrete cofferdam surrounding the entire site, with permanent steel cross-lot bracing, of the type shown here, to resist the enormous exterior pressure on the cofferdam.

Moran, Maurice & Proctor had become recognized for innovative solutions to foundation problems. One pertinent example was the Barclay-Vesey Telephone Building in lower New York City, completed in 1926. The basic challenge was that of planning foundations at a site that was originally in the Hudson River. Borings indicated that the bedrock varied throughout the site from 55 to 75 feet below high water level.

Moran, Maurice & Proctor elected to use a continuous concrete cofferdam surrounding the entire site and resting on bedrock. Construction of the cofferdam required installation of a series of pneumatic caissons before the open excavation began. The job was further complicated by the combination of hydrostatic pressure and adjacent street and building loads. Twenty-two caissons, each 8 feet thick and 40 feet long, had to be installed to depths from 55 to 75 feet to bedrock. In sinking the caissons, the contractors successively passed through fill, silt, boulders, peat, and running sand. The Telephone Building was among the first to use permanent steel cross-bracing in the foundations. This was necessitated by the unusually heavy exterior pressure on the cofferdam.

During the design of foundations for New York's Cunard Building in 1921, the firm was confronted with the unique feature of a site bounded on two sides by subway tunnels, with a third subway crossing diagonally beneath. Vibrations from passing trains required special measures to protect the structure. The diagonal subway tunnel also posed the problem of underpinning the building at the southeast margin of the site.

To complicate matters, the rock surface had a pronounced ridge at the center of the site, with a vertical drop averaging at least twelve feet. Previously sound rock had been shattered during the subway construction. The firm's engineers saw the best solution provided by foundation piers on each side of the tunnel. Trusses above, and independent of, the subway would assure that no vibration could be transmitted to the Cunard Building itself.

The solution to these problems was complicated, calling for a combination of open and closed cofferdams, the use of pneumatic caissons in part, and special underpinning of the foundation of an adjoining building. This was all accomplished without compromising the safety of the new structure and without having to underpin the subway.

At the time its engineers were wrestling with the Indiana Bell proposal in 1929, Moran and Proctor were involved with another telephone facility. The New York Telephone Company required an eleven-story structure in Albany. The technology for supporting a building of its weight on soil was not difficult. But in this case, the foundation design was dictated by two key factors that were not — unfortunately — concordant.

The first factor was the requirement that the building be free from settlement and any form of vibration or stress that would interfere with the delicate mechanism of the phone exchanges. The second factor was the nature of the site itself, a varved clay formation extending to a depth of more than 100 feet and so common to the location that it was classified by a regional name. "Albany clay," explained *Engineering News-Record*, "is well known and wholesomely respected by builders who have struggled with it, and many buildings founded on it have suffered serious settlements."[2]

The clay was deceptive. When first excavated, it frequently had the appearance of a dry, firm material that would be trouble-free for foundation work. However, when disturbed, it invariably became a soft, plastic mass. Analysis showed that it contained nearly 50 percent water by volume, with low bearing capacity. Any substantial load placed on the Albany clay would invariably cause marked settlement.

The firm devised an innovative solution. After numerous tests, including the use of models, it was decided to use a rigid foundation structure, with walls and mat supported by large Vierendeel trusses, sometimes referred to as "ladder trusses" because of their shape. They had been most commonly used in short-span bridges. The resultant structure was a continuous rigid foundation that could distribute the weight of the building to equalize settlement over its entire area.

The deep basement was designed so that the volume of Albany clay excavated equaled the gross weight of the planned structure. Thus the New York Telephone Company building became a classic example of the "floating" foundation, with a deep basement comparable to a ship's hull.

40

Caisson-sinking in progress during construction of the deep foundations for the Federal Reserve Bank, in the Wall Street district of New York City. At the time of construction in the mid-1920s, the excavation was one of the deepest ever made for a building.

Some Historical Precedents

From its beginnings, the firm has faced challenges that have imposed stringent demands. Many of the design innovations that resulted have influenced the course of foundation engineering. The following represent some memorable solutions to foundation problems in large buildings.

New York County Court House. The firm was selected in 1916 to design the foundations for this new court for a very specific reason. The site was possibly the most challenging in downtown Manhattan. It lay over what had long been referred to as "Collect Pond," a deep trough in the bedrock, where running sand persisted to a great depth. Borings had disclosed surprisingly loose sand and gravel deposits extending from 33 feet below the curb line to the limit reached, some 210 feet.

The building itself posed additional problems. Hexagonal in plan and 400 feet across, it was composed of six concentric rings of walls and columns that had to be uniformly supported. When Moran and Maurice made load tests, they correctly estimated that the underlying strata would support the load of the court house, but that settlements would not be uniform.

The solution lay in a unique base design that incorporated six concentric rings of foundation girders. Moran and Maurice planned this arrangement assuming that in a few cases the sand under two adjoining panels would provide almost no support. Thus they took into account the worst that could happen because of uneven supporting capacity. Each girder was so designed that it would transmit the entire load of any one column to the remaining part of that girder. Further safeguards were built into the job by varying the bearing area of footings to provide for variations in supporting capacity of subsoils.

Federal Reserve Bank of New York. The first consideration for the foundation design of this mid-1920s building was one of pure economics. The land was of high value, but zoning laws restricted the aboveground height to nineteen stories. Economics dictated that interior space be maximized on high-cost property. Since the height of the building was limited, the increased volume of usable space had to be obtained below ground. Thus it was that the Federal Reserve Bank design called for one of the deepest building excavations made to that time. Its basement was to extend five stories, 85 feet below grade and more than 60 feet below groundwater.

The character of the subsoil, groundwater conditions, the probability of disturbance from neighboring excavations, and the monumental nature of the building precluded any foundation that did not go to bedrock. Studies made by the firm proved that the unit cost of the building's space decreased as the volume of basement space increased. The design of the immense cellar area, calling for a series of 34 large concrete caissons forming a perimeter cofferdam supported internally by preloaded timber bracing, helped to bring the costs to an acceptable level.

Bank of Manhattan Building. "The builders of this huge structure," reported *Real Estate* magazine, "set out to turn over a completed building in one year from the day on which they received possession of the property." They accomplished this, "to the amazement of the building world,"[3] through unique and unprecedented methods, not the least of which was construction of foundations for the 71-story building.

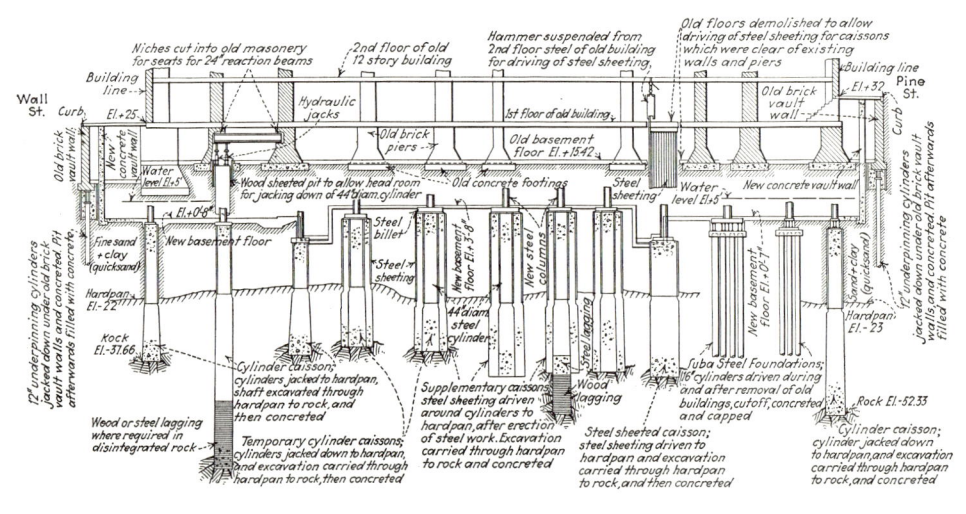

The complexity of foundations at the Bank of Manhattan Building can be seen in this diagram. The unusual foundation procedure in 1929 resulted from the demand that the new substructure be started underneath the old existing buildings at the site while demolition was in progress. By the time the old structures were demolished, the foundations were ready to receive column grillages.

The dual requirement of providing foundations to bedrock and at the same time keeping within the seemingly impossible schedule demanded new methods of foundation construction. The contemporary procedure of pneumatic caissons was discarded because it would have consumed five months of operation. The schedule problem was resolved by jacking steel cylinders to a watertight seal in hardpan. The heavy cylinders, averaging some four feet in diameter, were sunk to depths that ranged from 60 to 100 feet. After placing reinforcement, these cylindrical piers were concreted to the required height to receive column grillages.

One of the most innovative operations in driving the 262 cylinders to support the building's 104 columns related to their timing. The foundation contractor started his installations during demolition, instead of waiting until the site had been cleared of six existing buildings (three to twelve stories in height). Demolition and new foundation work were started May 1, 1929, and by June 16 column grillages were being set. This would not have been possible if the traditional caisson method had been employed.

General excavation below the original building level for the Bank of Manhattan Building.

American Bemberg Rayon Plant. Although the firm was traditionally involved with changing the skyline of lower Manhattan, it undertook different — though equally challenging — foundation problems in other parts of the globe. One such was the rayon plant at Elizabethton, Tennessee. During the late 1930s, it became obvious that the entire plant was in distress, its floors sinking, walls cracking, and roof trusses warping under settlement stresses. American Bemberg had been advised to abandon the plant.

The site was a foundation engineer's nightmare. When the firm's inspection team arrived in 1940, it quickly discovered that the entire structure was supported by a weakened alluvial overburden. This in turn was underlain by limestone bedrock that was soluble and broken, honeycombed with large cavities and channels. In numerous places, the overburden had collapsed into these cavities, forming sinkholes that extended to ground level.

Stabilizing the foundations for the future was vital because of the size and extent of the company's installations. These included a chemical plant, a precipitation building, and an energy station. The foundation engineers planned what was to be the firm's first of many large and extensive cavity stabilization jobs. A program for grout filling of overburden cavities was accomplished through drilled, cased borings. These borings were continued until three feet of continuous bedrock had been intercepted — insurance against grouting over a thin rock shelf. Repeated groutings, some under controlled pressure, not only filled existing sinks, but prevented the overburden from raveling into rock cavities and again causing depressions.

By the time the job was completed, all fluid lines had been tightened to prevent leakage and further solution cavities. Walls and footings had been underpinned, jacked, and secured in their original positions, the roof trusses had been repaired and squared, and the tall powerhouse stack had been permanently underpinned.

An Accepted Role in the Construction Industry

As the firm (now Moran, Proctor, Freeman & Mueser) was starting its fourth decade in foundation engineering, major changes were taking place, both in America and abroad. World War II was a grim reality. Construction operations were abruptly switching from peacetime work to wartime. The nation's economy was geared to a contradiction between huge expenditures for certain high-priority projects and meager budgets for jobs of less urgency.

Moran, Proctor, Freeman & Mueser had a legacy of leadership in foundation design and engineering which led to assignments in support of the wartime mobilization. It had now become established that the firm would focus its activities on difficult and unusual problems in the fields of foundation and underground construction, projects where the major challenge lay in geotechnical studies and engineering.

Following World War II and the resumption of peacetime operations, the firm found itself in a new surge of demand for services relating to buildings and industrial structures. These were to include office buildings, high-rise apartments, public structures, hospitals, schools, industrial plants, and many others. Typical services involved not only on-site construction inspection, but consultation, site investigations, enhanced laboratory studies, comparative cost studies for site selection, the inspection and correction of foundation difficulties, overall planning and field supervision, and the development of construction procedures.

The following jobs characterize the nature and variety of the firm's work from the end of its fourth decade in business to the present.

Medical Group at University City. A partnership was formed with Edgar Pardo Stolk in Caracas to engineer foundation projects in Venezuela, one of which was the design and construction of a medical complex for the Venezuelan Ministry of Public Works. The Ministry needed a 1,300-bed clinical hospital, a 300-bed cancer hospital, three research institute buildings, a nurse's quarters, and a number of support structures. These were to form the largest subdivision of the new University City.

Foundations for the United Nations Headquarters Buildings in mid-Manhattan were designed by MPF&M on a site consisting largely of reclaimed land along the East River. Shown here are the tall Secretariat Building (left), fronted by the Conference Building, and the domed General Assembly Building (right). The Secretariat Building was positioned on the site at the location of shallowest bedrock.

The firm was responsible for coordinating its work with the Venezuelan architects and planners and preparing complete structural designs and specifications for all of the buildings. The firm undertook a major effort to design a public building that would be earthquake-resistant.

United Nations Headquarters. The United Nations site was then the largest in Manhattan that the firm had ever been called upon to evaluate, consisting of six blocks along the East River. It was a challenging location for foundation construction, since much of it was reclaimed land upon the slope of the bedrock trough that has formed the East River. Only 100 years earlier, one limit of the area had, in fact, been a small cove known as Turtle Bay.

The boring investigation revealed dramatic variations in soil and rock, the most favorable location being in the southwest corner with shallow bedrock. With this factor in mind, that location was recommended for the largest and heaviest of the proposed structures, the 38-story Secretariat Building that today is a familiar landmark to world visitors. It was designed to be supported by concrete piers to bedrock. The General Assembly Building to its north was built on piers to rock, while the low Conference Hall, located along the river front and over Franklin D. Roosevelt Drive, rested on H piles, averaging 120 feet long, which were also driven to rock.

Mueser served as a member of the advisory board chaired by Wallace Harrison during the preliminary studies, a familiar function for which the firm had long experience and broad expertise. Subsequently, the firm designed and supervised installation of the foundations for the entire six-acre development.

Pittsburgh Complex. In the early 1950s, the firm was consulted on plans for foundations of two neighboring structures then being designed by architects Harrison & Abramovitz. The first was the 41-story U.S. Steel & Mellon National Bank Building. The second was the nearby 30-story Alcoa Building. The sites — both in the heart of Pittsburgh — posed a two-pronged problem: a congested urban setting and a tight, inflexible construction schedule.

Other on-site complications were heavy traffic, vulnerability to river floods, and the need for underpinning adjacent structures. Interestingly, the foundation for the U.S. Steel and Mellon National Bank Building was constructed from the outside in, and that for the Alcoa structure from the inside out. In the former case, the exterior walls were built within steel sheet pile cofferdams. As excavation of the four basement levels proceeded, heavy timber cross-lot bracing was installed and wedged. (This was one of the last of its type of heavy timber-braced cofferdams.)

In the case of the Alcoa Building, the center of the site was excavated first. Then diagonal raking braces were installed to provide lateral support for adjoining streets and buildings until the basements and exterior walls were completed. Both of these Pittsburgh foundations involved column loads that were carried to shale bedrock.

Court House Square. This project was recognized as "the world's hugest basement" when it was being completed in Denver. Begun in 1953, the excavation for a 5-story department store and a 20-story hotel

Denver's Court House Square under construction in 1956.

was the largest then attempted for contiguous buildings, extending for two city blocks at a depth of 50 feet. Its four separate basements were designed to provide more than twelve and a half million cubic feet of volume for parking garages, restaurants, sales rooms, storage areas, and conventional mechanical and servicing equipment.

The firm took on the combined jobs of making soil investigations, convincing the Denver Building Department that foundations could be safely designed for soil pressures exceeding those allowed by code, designing the foundations, and supervising their installation. One of the features of this enormous excavation was an extensive bracing system to protect adjoining streets and buildings during construction.

Chase Manhattan Bank excavation below structural steel floor framing used as cross-lot bracing.

Chase-Manhattan Bank. At the Central Office Building of the bank, interesting innovations for deep foundations in lower Manhattan resulted from the necessity of reducing foundation costs for the 60-story tower. There are six basements, down to 85 feet below grade and 60 feet below groundwater. Adjacent were deep foundations for the Federal Reserve Bank and the old Chase Bank Building, both constructed with pneumatic caissons designed by the firm.

The existence of a sandy till stratum under water pressure between the bedrock and overlying hardpan again appeared to require pneumatic caissons. Instead, the sand stratum was grouted with separate injections of sodium silicate and calcium chloride, preventing loss of ground from under adjacent streets, subways, and buildings and reducing foundation costs. No deep foundation has since been constructed in the area by pneumatic procedures.

To help reduce costs, the firm's engineers reused old caissons in the center of the building, which had previously been designed by Daniel Moran. The old perimeter walls were incorporated into the construction cofferdam.

Further savings were realized by the use of three tiers of permanent structural steel floor framing as cross-lot bracing. Pairs of girders were installed in each direction, so that the columns could be lowered between them. Stressing, to carefully estimated future lateral loads, was carried out by using four 300-ton jacks at each end of a pair of girders. The procedure allowed adjustment of the entire framing system to exact clearance requirements for future columns and precluded movement of the perimeter walls during transfer of loads from temporary to permanent lateral support.

During construction, a crane toppled into the hole and damaged the prestressed floor framing. This accident presented an opportunity to check the calculated jacking stresses. It was found that the full load in the damaged girders was transferred to nearby members. Replacement girders cut to predetermined lengths were shortened by packing in dry ice just before their installation. When they expanded, they picked up the original load with corresponding reduction of the temporary increased loads in the nearby members.

United States Capitol. The design of foundations for the east extension of the Capitol's facade was a prestigious and substantial accomplishment. In the late 1950s, to replace the crumbling sandstone facade and gain badly needed space, the east central front of the nation's Capitol was moved eastward by 32 feet. To protect the next interior wall, which could not safely support additional loads, the extension was designed with an independent interior wall. Intermediate floors were then cantilevered to the point of contact with the old wall while existing foundations were supported in place.

The new foundations were stepped down to 50 feet below grade, providing for the later addition of an underground garage. To maintain safe soil-bearing pressures, new concrete footings were constructed in pits beneath the existing outer walls. The new outer and colonnade walls were supported on continuous footings at a depth that required adjacent parts of the wings and central building to be underpinned.

Additionally the firm planned one of the largest underpinning programs ever undertaken in a single building, to make possible an elevator lobby and corridor connecting the House of Representatives wing of the Capitol with the subway leading to the Rayburn House Office Building.

Jacked underpinning piles, at the new lobby level, supporting a portion of the House of Representatives Wing of the U.S. Capitol, being inspected by William H. Mueser (right center) and *representatives of the Architect of the Capitol.*

Site of the World Financial Center in Battery Park City at the southwestern tip of New York City as it looked in the early 1980s during first stages of construction, with slurry walls that support the excavation and provide permanent foundation walls.

High Rises within Battery Park City. The firm is currently involved with four major buildings having six million square feet of office space in lower Manhattan at this 90-acre land site, which it designed in the late 1960s. Mueser Rutledge Consulting Engineers recommended, designed, and inspected the construction of perimeter slurry walls for two buildings at the World Financial Center. The 50- to 70-foot-deep slurry walls, embedded in rock to ensure a bottom seal, serve as both the temporary earth support system and the permanent basement and foundation walls. The firm's involvement also included the design of high-capacity, drilled-in caissons and closed-end pipe pile foundations to rock for the four major buildings at the World Financial Center.

Projects in the Nation's Capital. The firm is well represented in Washington, D.C., by a number of important current jobs, both private and public. One is a major office-hotel complex known as National Place, completed in 1983. Because of stringent height restrictions, many facilities of the Flagship Marriott Hotel, including ballrooms, had to be placed some 40 feet below grade. One of the problems faced by the firm was to plan the excavation with minimal disturbance to foundations of the adjacent National Press Club and National Theatre.

Part of the solution lay in utilizing a permanent slurry wall for a portion of the perimeter foundation wall. This procedure made it possible also to install six levels of parking below the adjacent office building that is part of the project. The ballrooms are protected against uplift pressures by several hundred permanent tiedowns.

The historic National Theatre is, in itself, an interesting foundation case history. During the earlier excavation for another building adjacent to the theatre, silty clay beneath the theatre had been stabilized by freezing. As the ground thawed, it became evident that extensive settlement would occur, followed by serious damage to the structure, if corrective measures were not taken. Called in by the contractor for the new building, the firm devised a scheme for pit underpinning of selected columns of the theatre. Although the thawing ultimately resulted in many inches of ground settlement, the underpinning countermeasures controlled the actual settlement of the structure to a fraction of an inch.

The firm became involved with the National Gallery of Art in Washington in 1968 when it undertook the site investigations for the new gallery addition. A few years later, it was again called in, as consultants on construction of the Gallery's New East Building. Hydrostatic uplift from high groundwater and the design of widely spaced main columns seemed to dictate unexpectedly high costs for the two basement foundations. The solution was a cost-effective system of grouted vertical tiedowns to resist uplift, rather than increasing the foundation mat thickness.

Mueser Rutledge Consulting Engineers is currently involved in Washington in the foundation design of the Willard Hotel restoration, the new Grand Hyatt Hotel near the Convention Center, the Canadian Chancery, 1001 Pennsylvania Avenue Project, and Square 290 — all along the Pennsylvania Avenue strip — as well as a new underground exhibition facility for the Smithsonian Museum and the Freer Gallery across the Mall.

USS Lexington *passing Golden Gate Bridge under construction in December 1934. Moran & Proctor was consultant to the contractor for the Presidio Pier and Fender Wall, Pacific Bridge Company.*

CHAPTER 4

BRIDGE FOUNDATIONS

"No other modern bridge has presented the unprecedented and fascinating problems in foundation engineering encountered in the design for the San Francisco-Oakland Bay Bridge. The very earliest foundation studies indicated that conditions here would require pioneer design."

> International Conference on
> Soil Mechanics and Foundation
> Engineering, *June 1936*

"The obstacles are insurmountable!"

This was the attitude that prevailed when studies were made of the feasibility of constructing a bridge from San Francisco to Oakland. The obstacles were very real: the formidable stretch of open water from San Francisco to the nearest point on the East Bay shore; the depth of water along the proposed crossing; the unusual depth to bedrock suitable for a foundation. There was no doubt that costs would be great. Even for an average structure, said an ASCE article, "half the cost of a bridge goes underground — is involved in providing the invisible substructure which supports the visible superstructure."[1] And this bridge would be anything but "average."

Once a commission had been formed and approval ultimately given to proceed with the project, it was several years before plans were complete and construction was begun in 1932. The major problem lay in design of the West Bay piers. Since the depth of water and to rock were far beyond the familiar limits of pneumatic work, another procedure had to be devised. The only available method of installation was by open-dredged caissons, but of an advanced design. It would be necessary to design piers with unusually large horizontal dimensions because of the bridge loads and the extremely heavy lateral forces contributed by winds, currents, and seismic events.

When the firm was retained to develop methods for construction of the foundations, it was evident that success of the design would hinge on controlling caisson flotation. All existing designs and methods had to be scrapped because of the hydrostatic forces at 120-foot water depths and the necessity of sinking the caissons to bedrock at a maximum depth of 240 feet, resulting in piers 50 percent deeper than had been achieved for any bridge in the world.

After months of studying alternatives, the firm evolved what was to become the "Moran Caisson." Fundamentally, it was a many-celled caisson of steel cylinders that could be reliably controlled through pneumatic flotation. The cylinders were capped by steel domes fitted with valves that controlled the introduction of compressed air and, later, the reduction of air pressure to permit the controlled inflow of water. The caissons had several other vital design features. They had a low center of gravity at all times to prevent uncontrolled tipping. Additionally, they had ten percent excess flotation so that at any one time ten percent of the domes could be removed to permit installation of additional segments to the cylinders while the caisson was being sunk to the bottom.

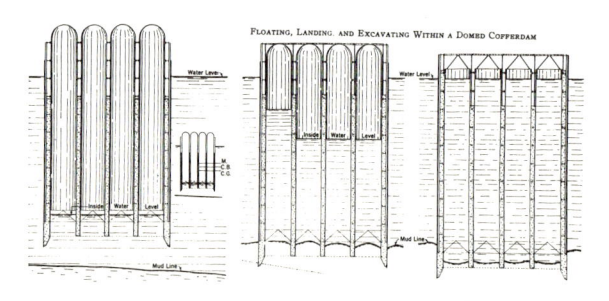

How the Moran Caisson functioned. Cellular caissons (left) were floated to the bridge pier site. The caissons were then "landed" (center) so they were firmly seated on the bottom, and (right) excavation begun. During excavation, some of the domes were removed for dredging operations while others remained in place to contribute to the stability of the combined units.

This reliable control during flotation made it possible to lower each caisson, as it approached the bottom, to an exact and firm embedment, and with much greater speed than had ever been possible with conventional caissons, thereby minimizing scour along the cutting edges caused by strong currents.

Setting Precedents

The San Francisco-Oakland Bridge has been cited often as a dramatic example of the art of foundation engineering. Yet its success depended as much on longtime experience and development as on the innovative techniques devised on site. Almost every step in the planning depended upon the consideration of problems that had arisen with bridge-building jobs in the past, some of them seemingly unrelated. The Benjamin Franklin Bridge over the Delaware River between Philadelphia and Camden is a case in point.

When this bridge was built in 1922, it crowned an entire century of controversy. The Corps of Engineers, which had jurisdiction over the river, recognized the risks and the real possibility of failure. From an

One of the engineering innovations that made possible the construction of the San Francisco - Oakland Bay Bridge in record water depths was the Moran Caisson, the top of which is seen above. After study of the location in the early 1930s, Daniel Moran conceived the idea of constructing cellular caissons with pneumatic flotation and false bottoms that could be moved up or down within the dredge wells.

When the Benjamin Franklin Bridge was constructed in the early 1920s, its 10,000-square-foot pneumatic caissons were the fourth largest of any that had been designed up to that time. They were built in nearby shipyards, on launchways capable of supporting a battleship, floated to the site, and sunk in place to form the piers. The caisson shown here in drydock is about 50 percent complete.

Although working in the chambers of the caissons under compressed air was rigorous and dangerous, construction of the piers for the Benjamin Franklin Bridge was carried out without a fatality and with a remarkably small number of minor injuries and cases of the bends. Careful medical examinations were required for all men working in the chambers, as well as for members of the engineering staff who were assigned as inspectors in the caissons.

engineer's point of view, the challenge lay in the design and handling of the huge caissons and the critical plan for sinking them into position. The science of caisson work was not new, but it had a long way to go in its development. As a spokesman for the Delaware River Bridge Joint Commission wrote in a later report, "Construction has been governed largely by rule of thumb, and experience and precedent more relied upon than any analysis of the forces involved."[2]

    The firm reversed this procedure. Its initial operation was the detailed exploration of the riverbed at proposed locations for the massive granite piers. This study provided advance warning about irregularities and unstable conditions, as well as the nature and depth of bedrock. As for the foundations, several designs were studied that incorporated multiple caissons in each location before it was decided that a single

Daniel Moran (right), with Ralph Modjeski (center) and George Webster (left) of the Delaware Bridge Board of Consultants inspecting the construction of foundation piers for the Benjamin Franklin Bridge.

large caisson for each tower pier would be the most feasible and avoid the problems of having to join separate units. One of the most widely recognized advances in the caisson design was in producing walls that were self-supporting, thus freeing the working chamber of the obstructions of cross-ties and braces. In addition, the toes of the caissons were much stronger and the cutting edges were more accessible.

Because of the improvements in design and the rigid procedures that governed selection and assignment of the workers and engineers during caisson operations, the foundation was completed without a single fatality and with a remarkably small number of injuries, all minor.

Many of the innovations and improvements developed for Benjamin Franklin Bridge were used by the firm in other early bridge foundations. The Vicksburg Bridge, completed in 1930, is a good example. It, too, required caisson work under compressed air for construction of a combined railroad and highway crossing of the Mississippi. The swift current demanded a unique method of anchor construction, special willow mats to prevent scour, and piers sunk to unusual depths of 110 feet. Deadlines were unusually tight, requiring much of the foundation work to be completed during the brief low-water season. All but one of the piers was finished during that period.

The bridge was the first to span the Mississippi in the 850-mile stretch between Memphis and the Gulf. One of several innovative features in completing the 2,931-foot main span was the use of one caisson as a diving bell to level up the site of the third pier, which carried the east end of the cantilever span and was located on a reef, part of which was soft rock and the remainder a very hard clay. "The riverbed was very irregular," said a contemporary account in the *Engineering News-Record*, "and the material was too hard to dig with a dredging bucket to level off the site for landing the caisson. Time did not permit rigging up a submarine drilling and blasting outfit to level off the bottom. Therefore the caisson itself was used as a diving bell."[3]

Questioning the Conventional

As consultant to the Port of New York Authority on foundations for the George Washington Bridge, Dan Moran provoked a controversy in 1926 by proposing use of deep, open cofferdams in 79 feet of water. Critics advocating more traditional methods were quoted widely on the dangers of the operations as proposed and the problems that would ensue. But Moran's foundation engineers had complete confidence in their recommendations.

"This bold resort to open coffer operations for so deep a foundation," reported *Engineering News-Record* later, "called for care and skill, but at no time were there experienced the hazards which it had been freely predicted would bring disaster. Well-conceived advance plans and construction skill in their execution made the work so rapid that it bore the appearance of being almost commonplace." The editors ranked the engineering job, completing masonry twin-tower piers, as "one of the deepest cofferdam operations ever undertaken for subaqueous foundations . . . an advanced development in this class of construction."[4]

Experience gained on the George Washington Bridge was put to good use when the firm acted as consulting engineers for foundations of a railroad bridge across Suisun Bay, northeast of San Francisco. In 1929, Southern Pacific Company decided to build a 5,600-foot-long double-track steel bridge with a 300-foot lift span. The project had already been delayed several times because of problems and costs anticipated.

However, as consulting engineers on the foundations, the firm convinced the company and the designers that it could reduce both costs and problems through unique but proven construction methods for the eleven piers supporting the main spans.

The first part of the plan was to utilize the open-caisson method for piers that would be carried as much as 135 feet below low water and rise some 206 feet from bedrock to the bridge seat. The second — and most unorthodox — engineering feature was the creation of "sand islands."

"The method employed in constructing the deeper piers is unique and of more than usual interest," reported *Contractors and Engineers Monthly.* "This has come to be known as the 'sand island' method."[5] It required installing a steel sheeting enclosure, 81 feet in diameter, around each pier site and then filling it with sand to low water. On the artificial islands thus formed, caisson steel cutting edges were laid and joined. Steel forms were then attached on top and concrete poured to the dimensions of the pier bases. As the weight of successive concrete lifts were added and the caisson sunk in stages, open wooden cofferdams were used to facilitate the operations, with their tops being at all times above high-water level.

This method of construction lent itself well to the need for foundations that would resist earthquake forces. Although the site selected was not intersected by an active fault, such precautions were deemed necessary because of the seismic history. Consequently, the piers were designed to withstand acceleration twice that which had devastated San Francisco in 1906. This development process was to be of immense value in constructing later bridges, notably the San Francisco-Oakland Bay Bridge in the mid-1930s.

Over the years, there were many other bridges that exemplified advances developed by the firm. One outstanding example was the LaSalle-Caughnawaga Bridge across the St. Lawrence River. Built during the mid-1930s, it held the distinction of having been completed a year ahead of contract time. This record was all the more impressive in light of the challenges facing the foundation engineers. Since the site was at the head of a turbulent stretch of the river, the Lachine Rapids, with currents reaching almost ten miles an hour, it was necessary to install the piers with a minimum of floating equipment.

A review of the problems suggested an unprecedented solution: constructing as many of the piers as possible from a trestle, providing advantages of a land-based operation. Design of the temporary trestle called for driving piles in swift-running water, regardless of river-bottom conditions and with a minimum of stream obstruction. The trestle, extending halfway across the river along the upstream side of the bridge piers, consisted of preframed steel tower bents held in place by timber spuds. Steel tower bents were also installed extending downstream from the trestle on either side of the pier locations, thus creating deadwater zones at the locations where the pier caissons were to be sunk.

The strategy of this trestle method was so effective that many months of labor and working time were shaved from the original schedules, with a consequent saving in construction costs.

Another job in the mid-1930s that utilized unconventional methods was the Huey P. Long Bridge over the Mississippi at New Orleans.

To solve the unusual soil and site problems encountered during construction of the Huey P. Long Bridge in New Orleans in the mid-1930s, the firm devised a new type of caisson with hollow walls above the cutting edges. Temporary cofferdams, of the size shown here, were used to protect walls and dredging wells outside of pier shafts.

Subsequently it was referred to as "the successful conclusion to a very difficult and hazardous undertaking."[6] The initial reasons for skepticism stemmed from depths of turbulent water — as much as 90 feet — combined with a very unreliable bottom of shifting, semifluid silt. This situation called for a seemingly incompatible set of designs for the caissons, on the one hand providing low weight to incorporate sufficient flotation, on the other, adequate strength to withstand heavy hydrostatic pressure on the hollow walls during sinking. Minimum weight was necessary also because the single-size fine sand of the river bottom had low supporting strength. Yet it was imperative that there be sufficient weight to overcome skin friction while sinking through a succession of sands, clay, and "gumbo" to the then unprecedented depth of 185 feet.

In constructing the pier foundations, the sand-island method, which had first had its test at the Suisun Bay Bridge, was employed. Two of its major advantages at New Orleans were that it eliminated the prevalent dangers of caisson tipping, since the work proceeded in easily controlled stages, and blow-ins under the cutting edges were minimized by keeping the water levels in the caissons equal to river levels. As for the caisson design, it was again a new type, extending the dredging wells virtually to the outer walls. This arrangement eliminated the traditional thick outer walls and permitted selected wells to remain unfilled. During sinking, each caisson was temporarily ballasted to ensure controlled settlement.

One of the most innovative, yet least evident, features of the New Orleans bridge was the research that was undertaken prior to designing the foundations. Applying new and not fully developed techniques, the firm made soil tests, both in the field and in the laboratory. These demonstrated that the bearing capacity of the soil was marginal, even should piers be sunk to considerable depths. It was for this reason, after testing with laboratory equipment of unique design, that the decision was made to use the caissons described, with large bearing area and minimum weight.

Another pioneering venture was the use of the bridge itself as a kind of on-site "laboratory" for continuing studies of soil settlement and compression. William P. Kimball, later dean of the Thayer School of

Engineering at Dartmouth, who was in charge of the firm's laboratory during this period of development, reported six years after completion of the bridge that "the studies of settlement of the Huey P. Long Bridge piers offer a comparison between theory and practice that is nearly ideal. The principles of soil mechanics were utilized in making a settlement analysis of this structure before it was built, and accurate and complete records of actual settlement have been kept ever since."[7]

The initial soil studies were begun five years before the bridge plans were completed, with borings as deep as 600 feet. These resulted in a preliminary report on the load-bearing characteristics of the deeper sand strata, along with estimates of the probable settlement of piers that would be founded above them. Further tests were conducted regularly, even when construction was in progress. Over a period of more than six years following completion of the bridge, continuing analyses were made of the observed settlements.

The research program, which followed the pattern of some of the early experiments by Dan Moran prior to World War I, pioneered the development of a soil mechanics laboratory that was to give the firm a special recognition. These studies led to certain important and practical conclusions regarding accuracy of the predictions that had been made before the bridge was built.

1. The order of magnitude of the pier settlements was accurately predicted.
2. The bulk of the settlement, approximately 70 percent, was correctly predicted to occur during the actual construction period.
3. Predictions of the magnitude and rate of progressive settlement following the bridge's completion were reasonably conservative.
4. It was estimated that some piers would settle considerably more than others during construction.

With the exception of the predictions for two of the five piers, whose settlement was underestimated by nearly 50 percent, the studies were remarkably accurate, especially since they were made with little precedent or past experience. It seemed evident from the results that a significant advance had been made in the art of soil mechanics.

In 1933, the firm was retained to design the piers of the Tacoma Narrows Bridge. The failure of the superstructure under a combination of sinusoidal and torsional movements caused by unusual wind forces spawned studies of the aerodynamic stability of numerous structures. The rebuilt bridge utilized the same foundations as those constructed for the original bridge.

Rendering of one of the caissons for the original Tacoma Narrows Bridge at Tacoma, Washington, shows the working elements of the 65- by 116-foot unit. These caissons were sunk to depths as great as 200 feet in currents up to twelve miles per hour. They were fitted with collapsible bottom doors to be opened after landing for dredging through 32 pockets. The two guy derricks removed muck from the bottom and placed concrete. The caissons were secured to 570-ton concrete anchors. These foundations were not damaged when the bridge failed and were incorporated into the rebuilt structure.

During construction of the Newburgh-Beacon Bridge across the Hudson River, one of the huge caissons being sunk to form one of the piers tilted about twenty degrees. The situation was remedied through a slow, meticulous operation that included the removal of obstructing materials at the base of the high side of the tall caisson and jacking at the low side.

The firm was also recognized more recently for experience dealing with the problems of swift currents and uneven bottoms. The location was the Newburgh-Beacon Bridge across the Hudson, during the construction of a new span in 1978. Four floating caissons designed by the firm for the contractor were being employed at the time, each of them quite narrow in comparison with its height. During placement, one of them, at Pier 7, began tilting to a maximum of twenty degrees and continued a slow, but definite, sinking rate. The firm assessed the problem and recommended corrective measures.

Armed with information from borings and having determined that the caisson was not damaged, the design team led by Sal DeSimone worked with the contractor and recommended the use of excavation

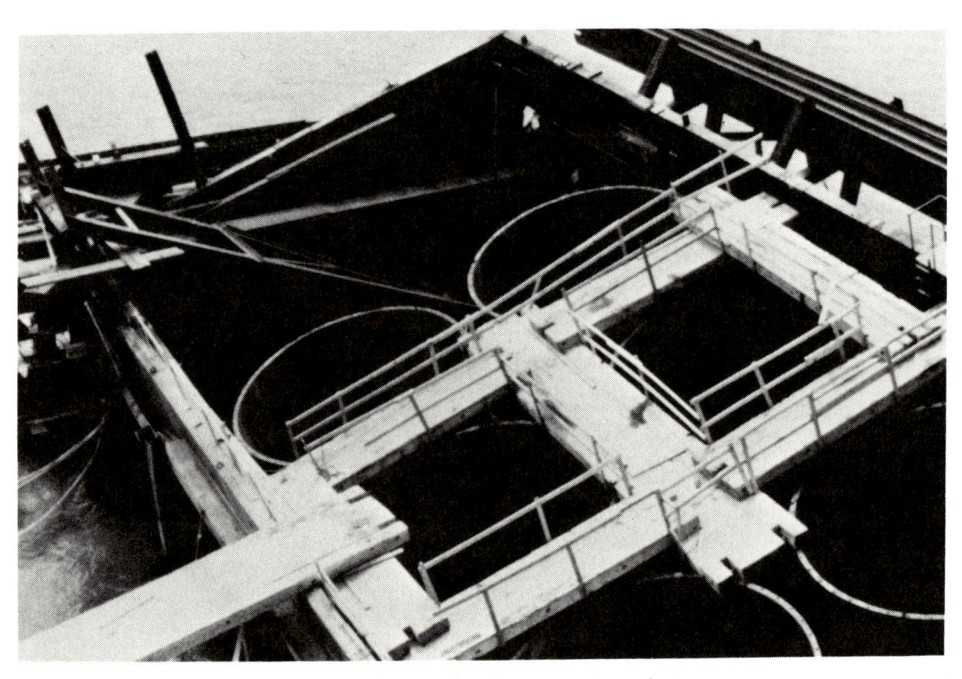

View of the tilted caisson of the Newburgh-Beacon Bridge, showing counterweight (upper right) and jacking beam extending to jack beyond photo (upper left) installed to right the caisson.

controlled from dredge wells under parts of the caisson and an upward jacked reaction to help right the caisson into proper position. The procedures called for careful design of all connections to the caisson to be used during the righting operations, to avoid damage to the caisson shell and frames. Correcting the tilt required several weeks, but was a good example of ways in which the firm has teamed with contractors to solve a construction emergency.

The firm has often been retained as consultant on bridges that have been damaged or experienced structural deterioration or weakness. Such was the case with the historic Augustine Bridge spanning Brandywine Creek and a reservoir in Delaware, which was closed when defects were reported after routine inspections. Investigations by the firm in 1979 to determine foundation stability detected serious voids in the supporting rock formation, as well as in three of the five masonry piers that supported the 700-foot-long, four-lane bridge. The firm recommended and designed a remedial drilling and grouting program. The bridge was reopened to traffic after completion of measures that included carefully controlled purging of deteriorated masonry joints, followed by cement grouting from vertical drill holes within the piers and bedrock.

Recent MRCE bridge projects include condition surveys on the Key Bridge in Washington, D.C., and numerous railroad bridges along the Northeast Corridor between Washington, D.C., and Boston. Foundation investigations were conducted for Howard, Needles, Tammen & Bergendoff on the Glade Creek Bridge in West Virginia, which spans a steep 800-foot-deep V-shaped valley. Assistance was provided to the contractor, a joint venture of Morrison-Knudsen Company, Inc., and Yonkers Contracting Company, Inc., on cofferdams and foundation construction procedures for the Greenpoint Bridge in New York City. A new four-lane highway bridge across Washington, D.C.'s Anacostia River is included in the Southeast Freeway Modification Plan for which MRCE is foundation consultant to the joint venture of the Fleming Corporation and DeLeuw Cather Company. The firm is providing consulting services to Parsons Brinckerhoff Quade & Douglas, Inc., including detailed pile-load testing over water, for the new Baldwin Bridge in Connecticut.

Washington, D.C., Metro, Du Pont Circle Station, under construction for the Washington Metropolitan Area Transit Authority.

CHAPTER 5

TUNNELS, SUBWAYS, HIGHWAYS, AIRFIELDS, AND OTHER TRANSPORTATION FACILITIES

"The largest public works project of its type ever undertaken in an American metropolitan area, Metro is a dual-rail rapid-transit system serving nearly three million people in the District of Columbia and nearby Virginia and Maryland suburbs . . . This time the National Capital region is setting new standards of excellence for the country and the world."

Civil Engineering, ASCE
September 1978

During the early 1950s, the firm continued from the office it had leased twenty years earlier in New York City at 420 Lexington Avenue, moving in 1955 to 415 Madison Avenue. It was now known as Moran, Proctor, Mueser & Rutledge, retaining the name of the late founder as a tribute to his innovations that were even then incorporated into foundation engineering's active methodology.

By the end of 1961, the firm was involved in the now-famous bridge-tunnel across Chesapeake Bay. Even in the best weather, the site was continuously under the barrage of heavy swells rolling in from the Atlantic. The firm served as foundation consultant on this four-year project, working with Sverdrup and Parcel, who designed the crossing and supervised its construction for the Chesapeake Bay Bridge and Tunnel Commission.

The overall plan called for a unique combination that consisted of four man-made islands; two trench-type sunken tunnels; three low-level trestles covering a total distance of almost twelve miles; two high-level, fixed-steel bridge superstructures; a 9,000-foot-long earthfill causeway; some five miles of new highway connections; and various substructures.

Despite the ravages of hurricane "Esther" and other storms, the foundations were laid according to plan in an exacting sequence that required meticulous coordination.

Meeting Transportation Challenges

The firm first served as consultants on tunnels during the World War I era. Two early examples were the Washington Tunnel for railroad traffic under Capitol Hill in the District of Columbia, and the Harlem River Tunnel in New York City, for which the firm served as soil consultants. One of Moran's most prestigious jobs of the day came with the building of the Holland Tunnel. This was started in 1920 and completed seven years later, the first subaqueous tunnel of its type and length in the Northeast. Moran, who had already established a soils laboratory in 1919 and was recognized for his pioneering work in the study of soil mechanics, acted as foundation consultant. He and his associates made test borings and analyzed the river sediments when the project was in its initial planning stage and continued investigations as the project advanced.

The firm's early experience in underwater tunnels led to consulting contracts for subway tunnels in major U.S. cities. During the 1960s came a series of extensions for the New York City rapid-transit system, whose initial subway had been opened in 1904. The firm was also called in as consultants for the Toronto subway, the first underground rapid-transit system in Canada, which was started in 1954.

The firm worked with various contractors in New York City on both the Second Avenue and the earlier Sixth Avenue subways. It also served as foundation consultant for the Baltimore Sewer Tunnel in 1975 and tunnel sections of the Baltimore Subway in 1976, working in both instances with tunnel specialists Singstad, Kehart, November & Hurka.

Many years of foundation research, planning, and consultation went into the development of Washington's rapid-transit system for the Washington Metropolitan Area Transit Authority. Since 1966, working with the general engineering consultant, DeLeuw, Cather, & Company, the firm has been serving as the general soil consultant for the new multibillion-dollar subway under the direction of three of the partners. The system, which eventually will be more than 100 miles in length, links the nation's capital with suburbs in Virginia and Maryland and is perhaps the most modern rapid-transit system in the world.

The work has required tunneling past many of the nation's most historic public buildings and has included three subaqueous tunnels, twelve unusual arched station excavations in rock, and a variety of innovative rail-transit features.

Having worked on numerous subway projects and transportation tunnels, the firm has established special credentials in this field of engineering so closely associated with deep foundation techniques and soil mechanics. Techniques developed on other heavy construction jobs are often applied to tunnels and subways. An example of this is the series of 21 ventilation shafts and emergency exits constructed in Boston for the Massachusetts Bay Transit Authority where MRCE serves as a soil and foundation consultant and provides specialized construction consultation on the slurry wall aspects of the work. One shaft is constructed through Long Wharf at the edge of the harbor and is 100 feet deep. The shaft is designed to buttress and protect the adjacent Blue Line subway arch tunnel as it is penetrated from the ventilation shaft.

MRCE is also designing four ventilation and emergency exit shafts in New York City and Jersey City for the Port Authority Trans Hudson Commuter Railroad Safety Program. These new shafts are from 50 to 100 feet deep and connect to existing operating tunnels. Needless to say, passenger safety is of ultimate concern to all parties involved with the work.

Expanding Transportation Networks

Drawing on its considerable previous railroad experience, the firm began a succession of consulting assignments for railroad improvements when it served as foundation consultant for the construction of an Amtrak maintenance shop in Boston and later as foundation designer for another in Rensselaer.

The firm has been serving as soil consultant for Amtrak's $2 billion Northeast Corridor Improvement Project for the railroad line between Washington, D.C., and Boston. Sponsored by the Federal Railroad Administration, plans for improvement of track alignment, roadbeds, and structures now permit routine travel at speeds of up to 120 miles per hour.

Among the various components requiring evaluation: some 900 miles of track with 855 bridges, 7 tunnels, 185 curve realignments, 16 passenger stations, and numerous related facilities up and down the corridor. Some of the projects involve interesting and unique challenges. One, for example, was the ancient Baltimore and Potomac Tunnel, 110 years old, that had to be modernized to serve as a vital link in the system. Located in Baltimore, it formed an 11,000-foot curve under the city streets, with clearances too limited for the handling of large, modern freight cars. The threat posed by the piping of soils from beneath the invert slabs often slowed train traffic to less than twenty miles per hour. The remedy required a lower, thicker, drained track slab, installed carefully — one track at a time — plus drainage and stabilization of the tunnel walls. All the work had to proceed with minimal interruption of the normal traffic flow.

Pier construction for a railroad bridge at Shaw's Cove, Connecticut, one of a wide range of projects on the Amtrak Northeast Corridor Improvement Project.

Other examples are the remedial grouting above the crown of an Amtrak tunnel 70 feet below the Hudson River, a 1,200-foot permanent tied-back wall in Philadelphia, and a stabilizing embankment in Perryville, Maryland. The last two were designed to correct long-continuing track movements.

Current transportation problems are often reminiscent of historic ones, demonstrating that there is seldom anything in foundation engineering that is brand new. In 1933, for instance, the firm was assigned a challenging task: build a double-track railroad viaduct through an occupied building without disturbing the occupants or some very sensitive instruments in constant use.

The structure in question was an elevated viaduct for the New York Central Railroad, running along the Hudson River in Manhattan. Its alignment would pass through a building occupied by Bell Telephone Laboratories on Washington Street. The foundation problem was in itself unusually difficult, requiring eight concrete caissons to be jacked 60 to 80 feet to rock between the building columns. This operation, furthermore, had to be performed with no noise or vibration, in order to prevent damage to delicate instruments and interruption of vital telephone research.

To control vibration, it was necessary for the viaduct's foundations to go to a base other than the sand strata carrying the concrete and timber piles supporting Bell's three adjoining buildings. The methods for constructing the new piers also had to preclude any possibility of settling the buildings through disturbance of their pile foundations.

The Bell Telephone Laboratories building as it looked in 1933 during construction of an elevated railroad viaduct through the lower part of the structure on the Hudson River side of New York City. Specifications and construction procedures developed by Moran & Proctor for the job required that all phases of construction limit noise and vibration to enable the day-to-day functions of the telephone research laboratories to continue uninterrupted.

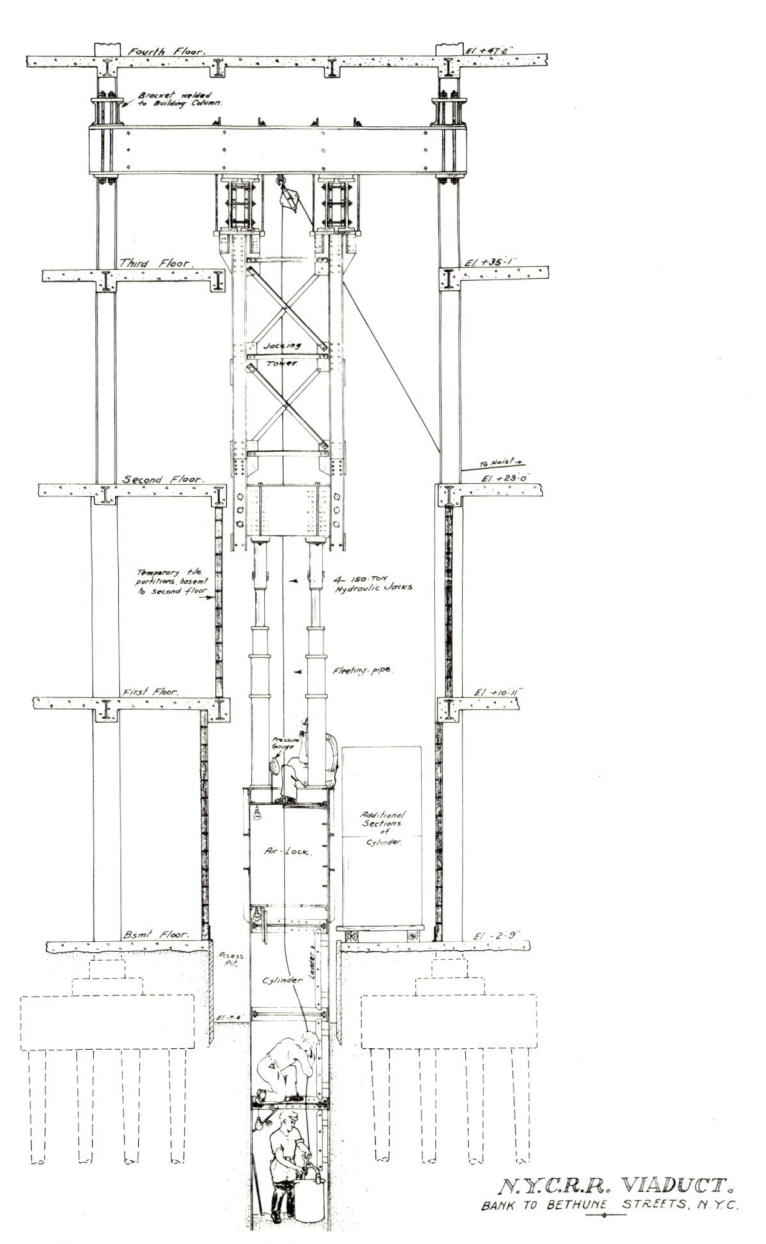

Diagram shows the installation of pneumatic cylinder foundations for the New York Central Railroad viaduct through Bell Telephone Laboratories in lower Manhattan. The man at the top, stationed above the air lock, monitors the air pressure of the lock in which two fellow workers are engaged in excavating the soil that will be hoisted up from the base. As they proceed lower toward bedrock, the cylinder unit will follow their progress downward, maintaining proper air pressure.

The railroad viaduct, supported on steel cylinders sunk as deep as 80 feet to rock and filled with concrete, had to be completely insulated from the building and its pile-supported footings.

Under the direction of George T. Gilman, project engineer for Moran & Proctor, all specifications were met and the viaduct became an integral urban link in the New York Central system in New York.

Highways

The firm's interest in this field expanded at the time it served as consultant for the development of the site for the 1939 World's Fair in New York. In that case, much of the soil analysis related to access roads as well as site reclamation and foundations for many of the fair's proposed buildings.

George L. Freeman, one of the principals in Moran, Proctor & Freeman, studied the budding science of soil mechanics and was particularly interested in applications relating to earthfill dams and highways. "When the engineer plans a highway," he told a meeting of the American Society of Civil Engineers in a hopeful spirit in 1938, "he can determine the stability of subgrade soils against frost heaving and softening when saturated, and the stability of embankments and slopes of highway cuts. If a section of the highway is over soft ground, the principles of soil mechanics will apply to the problems of settlement and safety of foundation strata against failure."[1]

George Glick, an associate who had joined the firm in 1926, expressed the opinion that highways were natural fields of endeavor for a firm that had long experience with so many different types of foundations. Nowhere, he pointed out, were foundation engineers called upon to evaluate and solve so many different soil problems as in the construction of a highway that passed over a multitude of terrain conditions.

One of the firm's ventures in this field was the design of the Indiana Toll Road between Gary and Hammond, completed in 1956 as a joint venture with Richardson Gordon Associates and Harry L. Balke for the Indiana Toll Road Commission. The thirteen-mile stretch contained almost 70 structures, including river crossings as long as 2,700 feet and elevated roadways up to 3,940 feet long. The firm was responsible for all soil testing of engineering properties and for design of all river diversions, embankments, and bridge substructures. It also conducted special studies to determine suitable and economical foundations for the structures.

Because of varying soil conditions along the route, there were diverse problems to be anticipated in the planning and solved in the execution. One example was replacement of a twelve-foot layer of peat with stable fill to control settlement along one section of the highway. Berms had to be placed along the road to prevent the central embankment from sliding toward the nearby Grand Calumet River.

Another major problem was determining the degree and nature of consolidation of soft clays common to the right-of-way. Tests showed that settlement was only slight under moderately loaded bridge piers, but could be severe under high earth embankments. In some instances these settlements could be as much as eighteen inches under fills 30 feet high. There was a danger that abrupt differential settlements could develop at bridge abutments. The problem was minimized by using lightweight slag from nearby steel mills in lieu of soil backfill. An alternative used was the equipping of bridge piers with removable shims, enabling bridges to be lowered slightly as adjoining embankments settled.

The firm's work for the Delaware State Highway Department in the late 1950s is historically of interest because of at least one of the foundation procedures that was applied to the job. The firm collaborated with J.E. Greiner Company in the design of three major interchanges, paving, channel diversions along the Christina River, and a number of structures and river crossings for the Interstate Highway. The Christina River Interchange lies in an area where soft, highly compressible organic soils were encountered in thicknesses of more than 100 feet. Foundation investigations and design studies were used to determine the most economical means of traversing these difficult areas.

One solution lay in the use of vertical sand drains, which had proved useful on numerous occasions for the stabilization of soft and compressible soils when the underlying soil was too weak to support a proposed fill. Interestingly, the idea was first proposed by Daniel E. Moran in 1925 and patented by him a year later. At the time, sand drains were described as "a method of strengthening a body of earth which consists in forming drains at numerous points in the area of the mass and compacting the material laterally also at numerous points to force the water out of it by way of such drains."[2] The first practical application of these drains was in the design of the easterly roadway approach to the San Francisco-Oakland Bay Bridge to stabilize the Bay Mud stratum beneath it. This led to experiments by the California Division of Highways and their first such application on highways in 1934.

This aerial view of the Christina River Interchange during construction of a section of the Interstate Highway in Delaware reveals the low-lying, marshy nature of the area. In order to solve the problems caused by soft, unstable soils, the firm had to devise plans to reroute the river at this juncture, relocate an adjacent creek, and provide extensive sand drains, embankments, and surcharge fills.

On another highway project, the firm's experience in waterfront landfill design was extensively utilized. This was the West Side Highway Project in lower Manhattan for the New York State Department of Transportation. From Battery Park City northward for approximately three miles, embankment offshore of the bulkhead line was to be placed atop a thick layer of river-bottom organic silt. The majority of the highway was to be constructed with depressed or covered roadway structures in this embankment.

Unique features of the job included design of wick drains driven through open water to hasten consolidation of the supporting river soils, protection structures at three Hudson River tunnel crossings, and the placement of project dredge spoil in retention basins within the embankments.

As general soils engineer with Woodward-Clyde Consultants, Inc., the firm performed a comprehensive scope of geotechnical and waterfront engineering services, including development of soil design parameters and foundation criteria and design of a 2,100-lineal-foot prototype landfill section.

Airports

The firm did not provide consulting services on airfields until the beginning of World War II when it collaborated in the design of Army air bases in Jamaica and the Bahamas and a naval air training station at Sampson, New York.

In 1944, the firm undertook its first site investigations for New York International Airport (first called Idlewild, then John F. Kennedy) and later assignments for La Guardia and Newark Airports. The Idlewild site was characteristic of much of the firm's investigations into airfields and a number of major land reclamation projects. Some 3,000 acres of the site were low-lying swampland: a meadow mat over organic silt, underlain by beach sand and a 150-foot stratum of glacial sands. Groundwater flowed through the sands into nearby Jamaica Bay.

The swamp meadow was overlain with fill, mainly in the form of waste materials that had been dumped at random. Unfortunately, compression had transformed the meadow mat and the underlying silt into a nearly impervious seal. Since storm water could neither penetrate it nor flow out laterally in adequate quantities, it simply collected in the fill, rendering it unstable. The firm took many borings, made consolidation and permeability tests, investigated the groundwater, and concluded that the fill could be drained into the underlying sand. Furthermore, the mat and silt could be further compressed and made to drain rapidly under loads.

Armed with these concepts, the firm designed sand-filled vertical drains that would penetrate to the glacial sands, with surcharge fills to consolidate the meadow mat and silt. Based on these procedures and evaluations, the airfield's surfaces and landing strips were designed.

Since completion of the airport in 1946, the firm has served as foundation consultants on more than 30 other airport projects, including domestic airports in Atlanta, Philadelphia, Washington, D.C., Miami, and Newark; foreign airports in Rome, Toronto, and Riyadh, Saudi Arabia; military air bases at Plattsburgh, New York; Ephrata, Washington; and Fairborn, Ohio; and special projects for such airlines as United, Eastern, and National.

Dry Dock No. 4 at Newport News Shipbuilding and Drydock Company near completion in 1981. The floating rig is installing the cylinder piles forming the dock walls.

CHAPTER 6

NATIONAL DEFENSE

"The design of Drydock No. 6, largest in the world, at the Puget Sound Naval Shipyard in Washington, was dictated by foundation conditions . . . Such jobs serve to emphasize the necessity for versatility on the part of foundation engineers as well as the usefulness of experience."

Engineering News-Record
Anniversary Issue, May 19, 1960

In 1975, the American Society of Civil Engineers listed the U.S. Navy Carrier Dry Dock, completed at Bremerton, Washington, in 1962, as one of 21 "Milestones in Construction History." Not only was this the world's largest and deepest in terms of volume, but it was situated on "made" land, requiring the dredging of some 600,000 cubic yards of soft soil and the placement of 1,200,000 cubic yards of select backfill.

Site selection was the responsibility of the firm, along with the preliminary soil investigation, the design for the entire project, the construction specifications, and a technical role in the construction management. Sinclair Inlet, site of the Puget Sound Naval Shipyard, and its surrounding highlands are characteristic of the Puget Sound Basin, comprising submerged valleys that are irregular and steep-sided. It was by no means the most compatible location for a carrier repair dock that was to be 1,152 feet long and 188 feet wide, with a 53-foot depth below mean high tide. In fact, test borings, soil permeability investigations, and other exploratory data suggested an initial change of site. The engineering recommendations were revised to minimize foundation problems that the investigations had revealed.

Certain designs were eliminated, either because of their susceptibility to foundation complications or their high cost. A gravity dock, for example, was ruled out — with or without piles — because of the expense. In the end, it was decided to design a fully relieved type of dry dock, using a drainage system under the floor and outside the walls. This arrangement served to control surrounding water pressures, lowering the water table and hydrostatic uplift pressures to a tolerable level. Water infiltration was limited by cutoff sheet piles surrounding the dock, with portions of the piling originally serving as cutoff walls for the cofferdam used to enclose the dock site.

Success of the operations at Puget Sound stemmed in part from the firm's earlier experience and achievements in planning and design of dry docks, shipyards, and port development. One example was the U.S. Navy Capital Ship Dry Dock that was completed at Bayonne, New Jersey, in 1942. At the beginning of World War II, the firm entered into a joint venture with three other engineering firms to form Dry Dock Engineers, whose primary mission was designing docks and related facilities at naval shipyards along the Atlantic and Pacific coasts. These included not only docks, but the construction of piers, foundations for heavy cranes, powerhouses, and machine shops.

The Bayonne project, completed under contract with the United States Navy's Bureau of Yards and Docks, was one of the major jobs. It held the record for almost fifteen years as one of the world's largest graving docks and the one with the deepest draft. One of the initial problems faced by Dry Dock Engineers was the need for rapid completion, under emergency conditions so demanding that the contractor had to begin work only four weeks after the engineers had undertaken the design. Within sixteen months, the dry dock was completed and taking "aboard" its first naval vessel, the famed battleship *Iowa*.

The length of time required to build a graving dock depends on several factors, not the least of which are size, availability of equipment, and nature of the site. In stable, impervious soils, construction can be relatively simple: excavating a cut in which the body of the structure is built in the dry and then flooded.

Frequently, however, the procedure calls for the construction of an elaborate cofferdam, a major undertaking that is both expensive and

The dewatered cofferdam for the Puget Sound Naval Shipyard Dry Dock. This carrier repair dry dock was considered the largest in the world at the time of its completion in 1962. It has a clear inner length of 1,152 feet, a width of 188 feet, and a depth to the floor of 58 feet below mean high tide and 61 feet below yard grade.

time-consuming. To avoid this alternative, Dry Dock Engineers applied the tremie method for one part of the Bayonne job, the 23-foot-thick base slab.

The firm had further experience with this method of constructing dry docks when it was called in to help develop the design for the two large graving docks at the Philadelphia Navy Yard in 1941. Here again, the savings in time and costs were significant.

Two other important defense jobs during World War II were the Bethlehem Steel Company Shipyard at Fairfield, Maryland, and the United States Army Air Base at Kingston, Jamaica, both completed in 1942. The former was under contract with the U.S. Maritime Commission for its noted Liberty ship program. The firm designed the two outfitting piers and sixteen shipways, and assisted in design of the power plant, substations, and a number of machine shops. At a time

Foundations for 25,000-ton and 35,000-ton presses at the Kaiser Aluminum and Chemical Corporation plant in Newark, Ohio, during construction in the mid-1950s. Foundation designs for such presses are complicated by special requirements, such as accessibility for service needs and resistance to vibration.

when there was great competition between shipyards engaged in the building of Liberty ships, the Bethlehem yard set a record. Barely six weeks after the design and construction contract for the yard itself was awarded, the keel was laid for the S.S. *Patrick Henry*, the first Liberty ship to be launched.

The Jamaica Army Air Base, a joint venture with the architectural firm of Holabird & Root, encountered basic site problems, since the locations that were the best from a construction viewpoint were the worst in the matter of health, training, and recreation for military personnel located in the Caribbean. The foundation engineers evaluated six different locales in all, before finding one that would be acceptable to the Army and the contractors as well. The job entailed not only the main airfield, but a landing wharf with full appurtenances; Army garrison facilities and storage, utilities, and transportation services; and the barracks.

Other Types of Defense Contracts

After World War II, the firm continued its work with the military services in the study and design of foundations for heavy presses. Under a program sponsored by the U.S. Air Force and the U.S. Navy, American industrial plants were selected to install these presses for the manufacture of critical components for aircraft, ships, and missiles. Some of these presses were more than 100 feet high, with pits 60 feet below grade level, dead weights of more than 10,000 tons, and forging capacities up to 50,000 tons.

Foundations for this kind of heavy industrial equipment require some of the same specialized knowledge and experience as that demanded for large buildings. But the similarity stops there, because of impact loads, the need for accessibility to equipment within the foundations, and special utility and service requirements.

Starting in 1950 and continuing for the next decade, the firm designed foundations for more than a dozen heavy forging and extrusion presses, in addition to serving as consultants for other major equipment installations of like nature. These foundations have been constructed in various types of soils and rock structures, far below groundwater tables. Several — where necessary — have been designed to be earthquake-resistant.

Foundations for such presses were designed for the Aluminum Company of America, Kaiser Aluminum & Chemical Corporation, McDonnell Aircraft Corporation, North American Aviation, and others. The largest was for the Wyman-Gordon Company in North Grafton, Massachusetts, with forging presses of 35,000- and 50,000-ton capacities.

The firm worked closely with the Atomic Energy Commission designing foundations in 1962 for the Bevatron at the Lawrence Radiation Laboratory at the University of California in Berkeley. The Bevatron is a high-energy research tool used in atomic energy. When it was determined that the unit's radiation output would be far greater than originally anticipated, the need arose for a substantial increase in radiation shielding. This in turn required construction of foundations to support an additional 11,000 tons of shielding.

One of the requirements was that the Bevatron, located high in the Berkeley hills, continue in full operation during the new foundation construction, in order to minimize shutdown time. After careful study of the operations, Sal DeSimone, the firm's representative on the job, devised tunneling methods under the unique, ring-shaped structure. Also required was a method for underpinning the inner portion of the Bevatron, to prevent settlements that might have interfered with the operations. This underpinning consisted of prestressed steel posts bearing on concrete blocks.

While this work was proceeding, steps were taken to prevent settlements of all adjacent segments of the huge unit, in which were installed highly sensitive instruments and accessory equipment. Researchers in the radiation laboratory perfected measuring techniques that could detect settlements as small as one-thousandth of an inch. It was significant that during the foundation installation there was no serious interference to operations and only one instance of a settlement of as much as a tenth of an inch.

During the "Cold War" era, the firm's team, led by Ted Kuss, participated with Anderson Nichols in an unusual kind of defense project for the U.S. Air Force and the U.S. Navy Bureau of Yards and Docks to erect a series of "Texas Towers" on the continental shelf off the northeast Atlantic coast. Similar in concept to the oil drilling platforms that had been erected in the shallow waters of the Gulf of Mexico, the towers were to be used as ocean bases for radar and communications equipment, with housing facilities for crews of about 80 officers and men.

There was one major difference. When the first of the towers was completed and positioned in 1955, it was the first such structure ever built for the difficult North Atlantic environment in locations where the water depth was as great as 185 feet. Background for the design required accumulation of masses of data on the oceanography, meteorology, and

Feasibility studies for Texas Towers of the type shown here, erected at Georges Bank, were initiated by the firm in the spring of 1954, and designs were approved for five platforms that were to have diesel generating capacity for electrical power, three independent electrical systems, a six-month supply of fuel oil, and a two-month supply of food and other necessities. The tower structures had to be self-contained units that could be floated to the sites and could establish ocean-bottom support independently. Wave and current conditions made it impractical to attempt assembly and construction from derrick barges.

geology at selected locations and in anticipation of ocean and storm conditions. Woods Hole Oceanographic Institute participated in developing these.

Another critical factor was time, since the late spring and early summer were the only periods when wave heights were relatively low and erection could proceed safely. The platforms were towed to sea completely assembled, including the supporting legs which allowed them to be lifted out of the water when they reached the site. The platforms were designed to be stable under the forces of maximum sea and wind at

Construction of the massive Vertical Assembly Building at Cape Canaveral, Florida, with an interior volume almost twice that of the Pentagon, required driving over 4,000 steel piles through a layer of hard limestone to bedrock at depths of as much as 163 feet.

their designated locations, to have minimal rotational deflections under all loading conditions, and to have a useful life of at least twenty years. Other factors entering into the design included fog, scour, corrosion, and the possibility of icing severe enough to cause abrasion on the platform legs.

A Trip to the Moon

Because of the Apollo/Saturn test flights and lunar orbits and landings, 1969 became known as the Year of the Moon. Mueser, Rutledge, Wentworth & Johnston were with these missions in spirit because of the firm's heavy involvement in the Apollo program, an involvement that commenced in the early 1960s.

Specifically, MRW&J was one of four engineering firms of the joint venture to plan the Vertical Assembly Building, described by *Civil Engineering* as "a standout feature of the entire [Apollo] program . . . a job so immense that it enters the realm of science fiction."[1]

The components of the enormous Saturn lunar vehicles were brought to be assembled into a complete space vehicle in the Vertical Assembly Building. The size of each Saturn was such that it had to be assembled and checked in its position near the launch site.

The result of the combined efforts of the four engineering firms was a steel-and-concrete structure enclosing some 125 million cubic feet of space — an interior volume almost twice that of the Pentagon. Design of the building required that the 362-foot spacecraft be assembled in a vertical position atop its mobile 46-foot-high launch platform. Furthermore, this huge structure had to be solidly anchored, resistant to vibration, and capable of withstanding hurricane-force winds at Cape Canaveral.

The very size and weight of the structure made the foundation design an undertaking of considerable magnitude when the site itself was considered. It was a low-lying, partially swampy area of undeveloped land with groundwater near the surface, and with tidal flooding rising to as much as 6 feet above it during storms. The geological profile comprised organic soil and vegetation at the surface, underlain by fine gray sand with shells and then clays and silts. A continuous layer of hard limestone, 1 to 2 feet thick, lay at a depth of about 115 feet. Limestone bedrock lay at depths from 146 to 163 feet.

It was determined that the foundation had to be carried to bedrock, using steel piles, and that foundations could not be supported on the clay or silt strata. Major design considerations were not only the downward thrust of the heavy structure but the uplift loads occurring on some columns when the building was subjected to winds of hurricane force.

The magnitude of the foundation installation can be visualized by the fact that some 4,200 large steel piles were required, with a total length of 680,000 linear feet and a combined weight of 21,300 tons.

The Renaissance of Dry Docks

Naval programming for dry docks and related facilities increased in the late 1960s. In 1968, for example, the firm made preliminary engineering studies for a graving dock and U.S. Navy ship repair facility on Guam in the Marianas.

In 1979, work was undertaken by the firm to rehabilitate three piers at the Naval Submarine Base in Groton, Connecticut, where Navy nuclear submarines are based. The piers had become outdated, not suitable for berthing the new attack or missile submarines. The construction phasing was such that only one pier was taken out of service at a time, leaving the adjacent piers to be fully utilized by the Navy.

Among other related projects was the development of grouting procedures to stop leakage along the 73-foot-high walls of Graving Dock No. 3 of the Electric Boat Division of General Dynamics. The job was planned in such a way that maintenance on Trident submarines could continue uninterrupted within the dry dock while repairs were being completed. The repairs included epoxy injection into the wall and sealing and grouting surface cracks in the interior of the wall with cement grout. Earlier, the firm performed a preliminary investigation for siting Graving Dock No. 3 and provided field inspection services during the extensive rock excavation of the initial construction.

As a result of these and other experiences in building and rehabilitating dry docks of various kinds, the firm's efforts effected considerable savings in time and costs for the Newport News Shipbuilding and Drydock Company, which required a major new submarine dry dock. Instead of designing more conventional gravity or cantilevered walls, the firm's engineers utilized 70-ton tiebacks anchoring 66-inch concrete cylinder piles. Aligned to form the walls around the

Construction of Graving Dock No. 3 at the Electric Boat Division of General Dynamics in Groton, Connecticut, in 1980. The photograph shows rock excavation within the cellular cofferdam enclosure and the construction of concrete walls to provide toe restraint for the cells. The firm performed site investigation and provided inspection and engineering assistance during excavation.

Construction nearing completion at Dry Dock No. 4 at Newport News, Virginia, a facility designed especially for the maintenance and repair of nuclear submarines. The firm was responsible for the design of the dock foundation and walls and the construction procedures.

540-foot dry dock, they provided a cutoff, which made a relieved-type dock possible. A second adjacent old Simpson-type dock was rebuilt to modern standards while continuing to service nuclear submarines.

A Major Line of Defense

Some 50 miles southwest of Columbia, South Carolina, lies a remote area almost as large as the City of Los Angeles, which is marked on the state map as "Savannah River Plant (U.S. Government Area, Closed to Public)." Initially developed in the 1950s, it was a much less known and less publicized "Oak Ridge," the site of one of the nation's greatest defense efforts in the design and manufacture of atomic explosive materials. The plant facilities in this closely guarded sector are carefully maintained and operated by E.I. du Pont de Nemours & Co., Inc.

The plant comprises hundreds of individual facilities, from tiny laboratories to self-contained power plants, a network of highways and railroad spurs, and large manufacturing plants. The region is one where some of the underlying soils are noted for their instability. The troublesome deposit is named the McBean formation, a soil formation which has often been found to include leached calcareous soils that contain voids and soft zones. This formation is a softer relative of the solution-pitted limestone strata that occur in large areas of the southeastern United States causing the sinkholes that are common from the Carolinas south to Florida.

Thus, it was a challenge for MPM&R when the firm accepted the assignment in 1951 to advise during site investigations and foundation studies for many of the facilities at the vast complex, in order to resolve any and all settlement problems. It was a singular trust for the firm, one of whose partners, Bill Mueser, was selected for the Board of Consultants.

MPM&R undertook two basic engineering responsibilities. The first was recommending design procedures for foundations that would safeguard sophisticated technical equipment and facilities. Such design was complicated by the fact that, although there are some 20,000 employees in the restricted zone, much of the nuclear production — even the operation of some large cranes — is remotely controlled. The second basic responsibility was equal protection for treatment facilities and the containment of hazardous wastes.

Site investigations were undertaken for a range of different types of structures, including manufacturing plants, transportation facilities, processing plants, and storage tanks for nuclear wastes. The firm recommended and undertook a very extensive drilling and grouting program to seal cavities, control and dispose of surface water and plant fluids, and prevent leakages into the ground. This ongoing program was developed in part through MPM&R's experience with solution-pitted limestone strata on other jobs, for clients ranging from the University of South Florida to a manufacturer in Tennessee, a knitting mill in Alabama, a chemicals corporation in Florida, and, in fact, Du Pont itself in several southern locations.

Considering the unstable soil formation, the firm's engineers recommended the use of mat foundations supported above the calcareous soils, rather than driving piles or caissons below these materials. This procedure has proved to ensure negligible settlement and has resulted in savings of many millions of dollars for the Savannah River Plant and the United States Government. As the manufacture of atomic materials and storage of waste materials has been modified during the years of plant operation and expansion, the firm continues to provide service in the foundation field to the operators of this critical facility.

Tieback installation for the bulkhead wall at the du Pont Corporation's Belle Works at Belle, West Virginia during 1966.

CHAPTER 7

MARINE STRUCTURES AND PORT DEVELOPMENT

"The bay is so much exposed that the violent waves often endanger the boats and make it impossible to deliver ore to them, conditions which have been changed by the construction of the mooring basin at one end of the bay, with its exit provided with a breakwater and wave trap designed to reduce greatly the size of the waves and secure complete safety to ships there and the opportunity to load them at all times."

Contracting
August 1917

It was not the most opportune time to undertake a major job on the west coast of South America. Shortly after Dan Moran entered into a joint venture to design an ore-shipping terminal at Cruz Grande, Chile, for the Bethlehem-Chile Iron Mine Company in 1916, the United States became involved in World War I. Shipping and manufacturing limitations, the isolated location of the job — 25 miles from the nearest town — and the temporary restrictions on the Panama Canal became pressing problems.

The terminal itself was an ambitious project for its day and remote location, comprising a loading basin, storage silos, viaducts, and shipping bins of 30,000-ton capacity, all protected from the elements. It was necessary for an entire camp to be established and equipped before the work could begin. The basin was excavated in the dry before the outboard end was opened to the bay. A part of the original rock was left intact to form a natural dike, along with a cofferdam of rock-filled cribs with a concrete face wall. This made it possible to excavate a considerably larger portion of the basin in the dry, removing some 35,000 cubic yards of earth and sand and 425,000 cubic yards of rock.

The operation was unique in that a considerable amount of bedrock had to be drilled outside the cofferdam. This difficult job, often accomplished in stormy weather and at the mercy of waves and tides, was made possible through the use of huge drills mounted in fixed steel towers, 65 feet high, on the deck of a barge. Despite all these difficulties and delays caused by the restrictions of World War I, the job was completed in three years

Planning harbor and port facilities in remote places, often under difficult conditions, has long since become part of the firm's history. Prior to 1959, for example, Kuwait City had long suffered a commercial disadvantage by not having either the harbor facilities or the channel depth to dock oceangoing ships. The firm served as consultant to the Kuwait government in a major project to remedy the situation.

As in the case of the ore-shipping terminal on the Pacific coast of Chile, the Kuwait job was difficult because of its substantial size and extent, remoteness, and inaccessibility to equipment and supplies. Prestressed concrete was recommended as the most economical and appropriate construction material, despite the fact that it had not previously been used in this area. During construction, it was necessary to dredge a channel to the wharf area, as well as to provide wharfage, crane facilities, warehouses, roads, transit sheds, and various utilities. In addition, future expansion of the wharfage was studied. The $26 million project was constructed by a joint venture of Hawaiian Dredging and Construction Company of Honolulu and J.H. Pomeroy & Co. of San Francisco.

Blasting operations at the Cruz Grande, Chile, site of the Bethlehem-Chile Iron Mine Company ore shipping terminal were complicated in 1917 by the remoteness of the area and the hardness of the rock at the site of foundation excavations. Rock blasted with dynamite and black powder was used to form a breakwater and cofferdam.

At the Bethlehem-Chile Iron Mine Company site near Coquimbo, steel drilling towers were constructed on barges, which were then positioned in the bay and maintained over the target area by large timber spuds. The hoisting engines helped to control lateral movement on the water — a difficult feat under local wave and tidal conditions — as well as to lower and rotate the drills. Drill rods and couplings had to be reinforced to overcome initial breakage problems.

Similarly remote and inaccessible was Macapa, Brazil, at the mouth of the Amazon River, for which the firm prepared a comprehensive report and complete plans and specifications for an ore-loading port. Completed for Bethlehem Steel in 1956, this port contains facilities for berthing cargo ships and large ore carriers; for storing ore and loading it into ships; and for repairing, servicing, and maintaining equipment.

The major problem encountered here was the instability of the riverbed, which consisted of low-strength, compressible silt and clay along most of the shore where the construction was planned. This instability was forcefully demonstrated when the riverbed was severely eroded by flood flow in the Amazon. The economical installation of fixed structures was not feasible except for one location where a pier and anchorage could be built on piles.

The firm's engineers under Paul Wentworth solved the problem by devising plans for a floating berthing pier and conveyor bridge. The floating pier, 810 feet long, was an innovative design that was patented. It was anchored by two long triangular booms whose inshore ends were connected to a heavy pendulum weight suspended from a fixed anchorage unit supported on piles.

The pier thus had the advantage of considerable flexibility to adjust to the seasonal flood range while supporting heavy vertical loads. The pendulums also provided an energy-absorbing system for berthing impacts of large ore carriers.

Other marine structures in far corners of the world include offshore bulk loading and ore ports in Cyprus and bulk-loading facilities to handle a variety of cargoes at Great Inagua Island in the Bahamas. In the last-mentioned case, the firm designed an articulated fender beam requiring special bearings. The facility is composed of dolphins, berthing, and mooring platforms in 50-foot water depths and a 1,300-foot conveyor trestle capable of surviving high waves and winds of hurricane force.

In the late 1970s, the firm, represented by Nick Koziakin, provided consulting and design services to Northville Industries for an offshore oil transshipment facility on the west coast of Panama for the transfer of oil

Bottom: View from the floating pier at the ore-loading port at the mouth of the Amazon River in Macapa, Brazil, showing one of two triangular booms connected to a fixed anchorage unit on shore. Top: The floating pier and conveyor, designed to remain stable even during flood conditions and turbulence at the broad river mouth.

Breasting dolphin and catwalk, elements in an offshore facility in Panama for the transfer of Alaskan North Slope oil from large tankers to shore storage and to smaller tankers capable of negotiating the Panama Canal. The firm's assignment included performance of subsurface and seismic studies for the facility at Puerto Armuelles, at the southwestern tip of the country, in the late 1970s.

The Trans-Isthmus Pipeline under construction across the Isthmus of Panama. The firm reviewed routes, made seismic studies, and provided design and on-site review when the pipeline was built in the early 1980s to provide alternative means of transporting North Slope oil across Panama from the Pacific Ocean to the Gulf of Mexico.

from large tankers to smaller ships capable of transiting the Panama Canal. Several years later, assistance was provided on the Trans-Isthmus Pipeline, which transports the Alaskan oil to storage and loading facilities on the Gulf of Mexico side.

Major Domestic Marine Developments

In the early 1950s, the firm began the first of many studies for the city of New York to determine the nature of subsurface conditions along the East River and the Hudson River. The studies, though general in nature, were to be used in proposals and recommendations for marine structures on, or marginal to, these rivers. In the early 1960s, as part of a joint venture for the City Department of Marine and Aviation, the firm completed a comprehensive study of the Hudson River environment. This study covered the Manhattan shoreline from the Battery's southern tip to 72nd Street. The report recommended the orderly development of the lower six miles of the Hudson River shoreline, not only for the use of harbor and port facilities, but for warehousing, manufacturing, housing, recreation, and parks. The study estimated costs for the basic restoration of key sites, especially through landfills to add substantial areas of valuable real estate to the city, and incorporated engineering and architectural features and requirements. Geotechnical studies produced extensive geologic cross sections and maps of subsurface conditions, which have been regularly used to plan new projects, such as Battery Park City and Westway.

Under a second contract, the joint venture prepared more detailed plans for berthing transatlantic and cruise liners at a Consolidated Passenger Ship Terminal that would make the maximum use of existing facilities in order to minimize costs. The proposed design connected three existing piers through construction of a new 1,200-foot terminal building along the bulkhead. The firm was responsible for making a physical survey of existing installations, coordinating all existing subsurface data with new testing, making studies for landfills and foundations, and providing structural engineering estimates for the proposed project.

For a proposed convention center in New York City, the firm investigated the site, originally located in the Hudson River over old piers and deep organic sediment, and designed a 1,000- by 1,200-foot platform supported over the water by precast concrete and steel H-piles. Responsibilities included planning and inspection of a $1 million pile load test program.

Some of the studies of the Hudson River environment benefited from earlier work with the city of Jacksonville, Florida, for which the firm had served as consultant on waterfront improvements for many years. After decades of neglect of its St. Johns River shoreline, the city decided to extend the waterfront development in an easterly direction to provide more parking and traffic facilities not far from the new City Hall. As consultants to the city and to the Atlantic Coast Line Railroad, the firm undertook studies of subsurface conditions for these projects. Recommendations were made for design and construction of the bulkheads for the land reclamation and facilities, as well as for protective measures for future construction along the riverfront.

Sheet pile cells being constructed for the permanent marginal wharf of the Tioga Marine Terminal. In a joint venture with the Ballinger Company, the firm was responsible for borings and soil analyses, as well as for the design of waterfront structures for this Philadelphia Port Corporation facility for ocean-going vessels.

In the mid-1960s, the firm undertook the first of a continuing series of studies for the Philadelphia Port Corporation to evaluate six potential sites for marine terminals on the Delaware River. Borings and soil testing and analyses were performed for each site, leading to comparative construction cost estimates for wharves at the six selected locations. As a result of this initial investigation, the firm was engaged, in the early 1970s, in a joint venture with the Ballinger Company of Philadelphia to design the city's new Tioga Marine Terminal, with container and mixed-cargo loading and unloading facilities. The firm's team, led by Max Bernheimer, designed this terminal to accommodate oceangoing vessels with drafts as deep as 40 feet. The project provided seven berths at a 3,180-foot wharf and bulkhead structure, and a landfill, 600 feet wide, for roads, railroad facilities, cargo handling, and utilities.

One of the advantages of the recommended site was that the subsoil conditions were highly favorable and convenient borrow areas for fill were nearby. Because of the predominantly fresh water in this location and consequently a less corrosive environment, the use of sheet-pile cells for the permanent marginal structure, with inshore fills, was a natural choice. The wharf and the bulkhead structures were built on 78 sheet-pile cells, each 51 feet in diameter.

Thirty-five years earlier, in 1937, the firm had specified what was probably the first use of this kind of permanent cellular construction when it had been commissioned to design the Sparrows Point Ore Dock in Baltimore Harbor.

The Economics of Waterfront Development

Cost-saving has, historically, been one of the major objectives of soil engineering and site investigation, second only to assuring the longtime reliability of the foundations themselves and their safe construction. Such savings have often been achieved by the selection of the most favorable site and the use and development of landfills.

One pertinent example was the firm's planning of the 137-acre Ambrose Marine Terminal in Stapleton, Staten Island, on upper New York Bay. The facilities included a marginal wharf capable of supporting container-handling cranes, landfills to create adequate upland area, buildings, and ancillary facilities appropriate for operation of a terminal to service general cargo and container ships. For this project, MRW&J conducted preliminary site investigations, including the inspection of existing facilities and geotechnical studies. The resulting report discussed alternative designs and proposed an expansion of the planned landfill that would sharply reduce both the construction and the annual maintenance costs, while actually doubling the available acreage.

Favorable use of landfill has become a science in itself, especially in the planning and development of port facilities in locations with challenging subsoil problems. The Northeast Marine Terminal, located on Gowanus Bay in Brooklyn, is typical.

When the firm was called in to investigate the site in 1969, it found highly unfavorable subsoils, including varying thicknesses of harbor mud, a thin stratum of sand over most of the area, and a deep underlying stratum of varved silt and clay — the classic "Bull's Liver." In some areas, the sand stratum had been eroded during postglacial times by a stream that had cut diagonally across the site and removed the desirable bearing layer.

The firm concluded that a marine terminal of this type, where the interior is used for container storage, could utilize essentially debris fills and yet be minimally affected by substantial settlement of fill surfaces. Construction costs were minimized by eliminating some of the usual excavation and disposal of compressible soils and at the same time procuring low-cost fill materials, such as spoil from nearby construction. This was the method used for the interior areas, systematically overfilling to reduce future settlements.

Three separate types of enclosing perimeter structures were required to adapt to upland conditions. Along the major wharf supporting the heaviest container crane, a relieving platform was built, supported on a combination of new piles and existing timber piles salvaged in place from an earlier pier. On the second face of the terminal, the most economical perimeter was an installation of sheet-pile cells, with a double row at the glacially eroded channel where the underlying soils were weak. On the

Closeup showing the offshore mooring facilities near Northport, Long Island, for unloading fuel from ocean-going oil tankers. The firm designed a special fendering system so that operations could continue uninterrupted even during moderately rough weather.

Aerial view of the Northport offshore fuel unloading facility shows the relatively small size of the total unit. Studies of currents, tidal conditions, and the seabed in this southwestern area of Long Island Sound were required for design of this mooring system.

third side, underlain by mud, a stabilizing berm of small stone was specified, to support the bottom of a steel sheet-pile cutoff wall. The top of the sheeting was supported against an existing pier deck.

Among other marine structures and port facilities to which the firm has contributed its manpower and expertise are the Northport Offshore Fuel Unloading Terminal for the Long Island Lighting Company, which has an innovative fendering design and a combined fixed and anchor mooring system; an oil unloading terminal near Riverhead, New York, for Northville Industries, which when designed was the only port on the East Coast capable of berthing 200,000-ton supertankers; a desalination plant in Saudi Arabia, which includes 30,000 lineal feet of breakwaters designed to withstand 13-foot-high waves; breakwaters in El Salvador which required new construction procedures to compensate for weather-related damage to the riprap seawalls and cofferdams; Ocean One, a three-story shopping mall, built on a platform extending into the surf zone in Atlantic City; and port and terminal facilities for major corporations: Du Pont, Kaiser, United Fruit Company, Bethlehem Steel, Moore McCormack Lines, Todd Shipbuilding Corporation, Con Edison, and TransAmerica Trailer Transport.

Currently the firm is active at the Port of Albany, a deepwater port 130 miles up the Hudson River from New York City. An MRCE survey and inspection of existing facilities for the Albany Port District Commission, completed in 1985, developed concepts for required remedial measures. The port structures requiring repair or replacement are supported on untreated timber piles installed in 1927. The study has shown that these piles are virtually free of rot and borer infestation. Float ice forced under the wharves by ships has damaged the outboard piles, causing movement and in some cases initiating wharf collapse. Design documents are being prepared for pile replacement under the sections of the wharves which have not collapsed to maintain wharves in use and avoid the capital costs of total replacement, thereby keeping the port competitive with other East Coast ports.

Overview of the Lower Colorado River Dam at Austin, Texas, showing extensive reconstruction under way in the late 1930s. The dam had been seriously damaged by floods three times since its original construction in 1894, and core borings to 200 feet showed extensive undermining and poor foundation rock. The basic structure of the dam was salvaged through extensive grouting and embodied in the new structure.

CHAPTER 8

DAMS, RESERVOIRS, POWER PLANTS, AND WASTE TREATMENT

"Contractors could use geotechnical engineers and their expertise more intelligently than they do. Contractors should have geotechnical engineers on their staffs, or should retain them as consultants. But they don't. They use their own judgement as to safe side-slope angle, for instance. Then they retain geotechnical people to support claims after a problem has arisen."

> Civil Engineering
> *March 1981*

When it was completed in 1894, the Lower Colorado River Dam three miles northwest of Austin, Texas, was an impressive accomplishment for its era. More than 1,000 feet long, it was the highest masonry overfall dam in the world. Its construction had been a classic example of dedication and determination, as the engineers contended with frequent floods; porous, faulted limestone with unforeseen springs and underseepage; and several failures of headgate masonry. Nevertheless, the completed dam, standing 60 feet high above low water, provided a badly needed source of water for the nearby city, while its four horizontal turbines contributed 2,400 horsepower to drive electric generators.

Six years after completion, the dam was in ruins.

In April 1900, the spillway failed during a severe flood that was running more than ten feet over the crest. A length of 500 feet slid out, in two sections that remained upright and stood at almost their original level.

It was fifteen years before the face was rebuilt, after many accidents and interruptions. Yet, within less than a year, the dam was again useless, after another flood carried away twenty crest gates and left the tailrace and draft tubes of the powerhouse blocked with debris. Subsequent engineering investigations were made with little result, especially after another flood tore out most of the crest gate piers and left the site a shambles.

Such were the conditions when, in 1937, the Lower Colorado River Authority proposed to rebuild the structure as one unit in its series of power dams on the river. The Authority asked the firm (then Moran, Proctor, Freeman & Mueser) to make a thorough investigation of the site and structure and — if possible — outline a plan of reconstruction.

"The entire history of the structure," reported George L. Freeman, "illustrates a half century's advance in engineering practices and construction methods applied to foundations in bad rock." As he pointed out, the site lay in a fault zone to begin with, where the underlying rock varied from soft to very hard, was extensively fractured, and was traversed by solution channels, caverns, and water flow from various springs.

"In the face of these conditions," he said, "the original dam had been founded virtually on the surface of the riverbed rock. This fact, together with the absence of grouting and with deficient superstructure design, gave rise to most of the trouble that marked the history of the dam."[1]

The firm's investigations included core borings to 200-foot depths, investigations by divers, soundings, and tests of materials. Large areas of the dam were shown to be severely undermined, with the structure supported only by occasional pinnacles of rock.

An outstanding feature of the reconstruction was the plan to salvage the devastated ruins that existed. This was accomplished by a number of procedures that included the extensive cutting and removal of rock and old masonry with pneumatic hammers, grouting to form an impervious curtain beneath the dam and dikes, and reconstruction of the downstream toe to prevent further erosion. When reconstruction was completed in 1940, the dam not only provided a reliable water supply for the city of Austin but was able to develop more than eight times the horsepower of the earlier turbines.

The firm's experience in design and construction of dams was based on jobs going back almost to its founding. During the previous 30 years, it had worked as consultants on many important dams, reservoirs, and power plants, from the gathering of original data through site selection and the supervision of construction. Included in these categories were dams for the Arkansas Light & Power Company and the Arkansas Water Company; the Saskatoon Dam in western Canada; the Cerro de Pasco and Mantaro River dams in Peru; the Baker River Dam in the Puget Sound basin; a dam, canal, and lock for the Svirstroy Hydro-electric Development in Russia; the Chickamauga Dam for the Tennessee Valley Authority; locks on the Allegheny River; power facilities for the Illinois Light & Power Company; and tidal gates and basins for the New York World's Fair.

Developments in Procedures

Earth-fill dams, although historically among the oldest forms, were often constructed by random methods, depending upon the types of borrow material available. But the firm approached such projects scientifically, using soil mechanics and testing as a basis for its recommendations and planning.

One excellent example of the application of soil mechanics principles is the earth-filled dam and dike for plant water supply in Bahia, Brazil, in 1952. Constructed for the Lone Star Cement Corporation, these units were part of a reservoir development designed to store process water for cement-plant operations during an eight-month

The Oroville Dam, shown under construction here on the Feather River in northern California in the mid-1960s, exemplifies the kind of foundation project for which extensive studies of the soil and environment can result in the effective utilization of vast quantities of local materials for the job itself. One of the major challenges faced by the firm was the study of unique combinations of boulders and gravel, whose suitability for fill could be determined only by using specially devised testing equipment at the site.

dry season. The best available site was underlain by soft, silty shale and a layer of medium to stiff clay. Extensive soil tests of these materials were conducted in the firm's laboratory in New York City.

Remoteness of the site made it impractical to consider any construction materials except the clay and sand that were locally available. Since the clay was excessively plastic and subject to shrinkage upon drying, it was used only where it could be kept continuously wet. A zoned cross section was designed, utilizing an impervious clay core with outer shells of relatively pervious sand. The impermeability of the clay made it possible to specify a core only 17½ feet thick at the crest and 46 feet at the base. Key to successful construction was the rigid control throughout of the moisture content in all materials used.

Some ten years later, Philip C. Rutledge began serving as consultant for another earth-filled dam, the largest of its type in the United States. This was the Oroville Dam on the Feather River, completed by the California Department of Water Resources in 1968 as one of its major

The Akosombo Dam under construction on the Volta River in Ghana in 1960. This dam, like the one at Oroville, California, is an example of the application of soil mechanics and foundation studies to determine how best to make use of local materials and minimize the cost of transportation of fill for a structure subject to seismic activity.

irrigation projects. With a central core embankment 756 feet high and extending 6,800 feet in length, the dam required the movement of more than 80 million cubic yards of suitable fill materials before completion.

Unusual problems were faced in designing this dam, both because of its unprecedented size and height and because of local seismicity. Research and soil investigations were complicated, too, because of the unusual nature of some of the materials considered for use in the dam. Vast fields of placer-mining gravel downstream of the site were likely sources for the shells. However, since much of the gravel contained boulders, large-sized testing equipment and high-pressure tests had to be devised to determine accurately the strength and deformability of the shell.

This kind of geotechnical research is not necessarily always conducted for a specific construction project. For example, the firm has had a long relationship with the California Department of Water Resources, often advising on tests in the field or conducting them in its soil laboratory. For the United States Soil Conservation Service, the firm has undertaken two special research studies, one on the use of weathered shale as a borrow for earth dams, the other studying the extension strains of low-level outlet pipes placed beneath earth dams.

High Dams — and Low Ones

The firm has acted as consultants for a number of dams in zones plagued by strong earthquakes and other threatening natural forces. One was the Akosombo Dam on the Volta River in Ghana, completed for commercial operation in 1965. The world's seventh highest rock-fill dam at that time, it created the fifth largest lake in Africa, a reservoir covering 3,275 square miles. It was designed by Kaiser Engineers to supply electricity for aluminum production, as well as to satisfy domestic power requirements for the entire nation. A typical problem was the selection of materials that were both suitable and available locally in enormous quantities. The solution in this case was a rock fill with a central clay core, designed so that the regional seismic activity would not endanger the structure.

Similar problems and solutions are characteristic worldwide, as the firm has discovered when serving as consulting engineers on dams and power facilities in such far-flung corners of the globe as Brazil, Canada, Colombia, India, Italy, Mexico, Nicaragua, Pakistan, Panama, and Puerto Rico.

Time and distance are always problems as well, since many dams, reservoirs, and power projects are years in the planning and many years more in the implementation. Such was the case with the Salto Grande Project in South America. This project was debated for more than twenty years before any active investigation took place in the early 1970s, mainly in the nature of limited subsurface exploration, with little progress on the design of the long, low earth embankments. Salto Grande was conceived as a dam and lock on the Uruguay River, which separates Uruguay from Argentina, with power stations on both sides and long earth embankments beyond the powerhouses.

By 1974, when the firm had been brought in as engineering consultants, work had commenced only on the Uruguayan side. Representing the firm, Philip Rutledge made trips to the site for extended studies over the next five years, recommending certain changes in the central clay core and the gravel filter layers and outer rock coverings. Selection of materials was dictated by the availability and cost of local materials. Nevertheless, the details were worked out satisfactorily, and within practical safety margins. Even after long sections of low-height embankment were being completed in part of the project, it was evident that careful inspections would have to be made for a year or more to check for underseepage and to evaluate performance characteristics.

Small dam projects can be more rewarding for the consulting engineer who can study the problems, evolve the answers, and see them implemented within a reasonable time. Yet these jobs can test ingenuity and patience. A case in point was the rehabilitation of Lake Purdy Dam on the Little Cahaba River in Selby County, Alabama, owned by the city of Birmingham. It was a modest structure when built, prior to World War I, 73 feet high, 445 feet long, with a storage capacity of about six billion gallons.

During construction, numerous cavities in the bedrock were backfilled with concrete. After the reservoir was filled, leaks began to appear, increasing with each year of service and requiring extensive countermeasures to reduce the underseepage. In 1927, the dam was raised twenty feet and an asphalt grouting program was undertaken to prevent failure under this increased head. By 1974, however, the leakage was increasing so significantly that the Corps of Engineers declared the dam unsafe and recommended that remedial measures be undertaken.

When the firm was called in by Malcolm Pirnie, Inc., to assist in a rehabilitation program in 1979, it was with the knowledge that the Lake Purdy Dam had a history of almost 70 years of chronic leakage and other problems. However, a detailed review of the original construction methods and the later repair efforts indicated generally where the problems lay. It was decided that a grouting program was the best

LAKE PURDY DAM

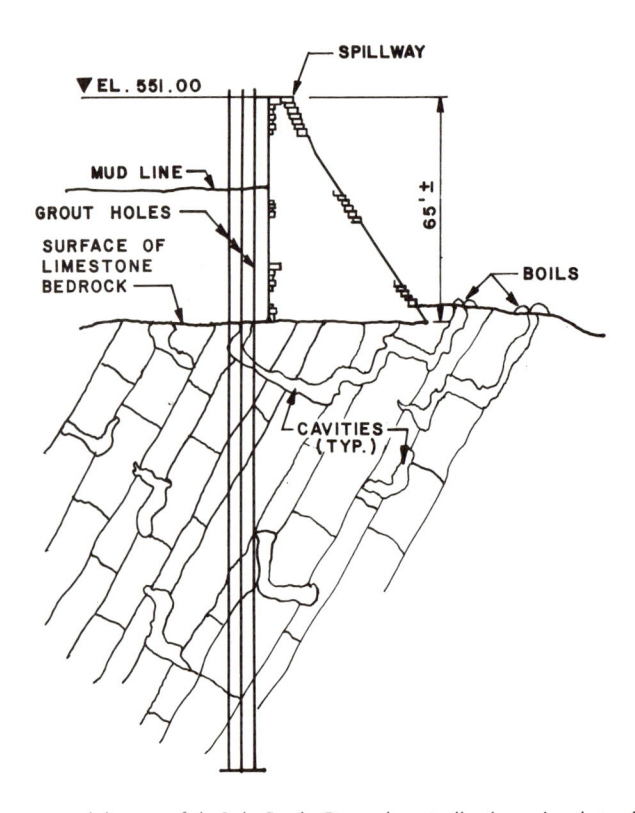

Cross-sectional diagram of the Lake Purdy Dam schematically shows the relationship of the grout holes to the fracture and cavity pattern in the bedrock.

solution, since it could simultaneously explore the location and nature of cavities and grout them as they were encountered, using different grout mixes and formulations to seal the various trouble spots.

The inaccessibility of many parts of the reservoir dictated the use of drilling barges. Borings and corrective measures were hindered by chert concretions in the bedrock hard enough to dull drill bits, and by pockets of asphaltic materials placed during previous rehabilitation attempts, which clogged and bound core drills and tubes. The fractured nature of the rock made it difficult to keep boreholes open. In addition, there were so many cavities and holes that the air pressure to operate the drills often ejected materials long distances away from where the drilling was in progress.

Rehabilitation under way at the Lake Purdy Dam in Birmingham, Alabama, in 1980, to correct the daily leakage of some six million gallons from the city's major water supply. The firm recommended and applied a drilling and grouting program that successfully solved the problems of the 70-year-old dam.

One effective procedure was the use of dye that was injected as a tracer into various grout holes. By noting the intensity of color and time required for the dye to exit downstream, it was possible to trace the path of grout, as well as to determine whether the procedure was starting to seal a cavity or simply losing materials. Conventional grouting materials proved ineffective, despite the use of various bulking agents, the addition of cement, and experiments with coarser granular materials, such as crushed stone and gravel. Most washed right through the cavities and emerged at the downstream boils, despite temporary sandbagging to slow the water flow.

The eventual solution was the use of slag from open-hearth furnaces. It was light enough to be washed into cavities, interlock itself in the holes, and yet remain soft enough for redrilling. When cavity packing with slag followed by cement grouting began there was a dramatic drop in the flow and underseepage. Furthermore, the tendency of the slag to cling to the crevices and cavities made it possible to use extra pressure to flush clay, mud, and old grout from the seams — materials that would later have eroded and caused the same problems all over again.

Currently, the firm is collaborating with Hazen and Sawyer in the design and construction inspection of two earth-fill dams over 100 feet in height in the North Carolina Piedmont for the cities of Durham and Chapel Hill. Both of the structures are built in deeply weathered crystalline rocks where all of the materials from the required excavations are utilized in zoned cross sections, with the residual soil in the central core and the more rock-like materials placed in the shells.

Power Plants

The firm has long been active in assisting utilities in expanding their generating capacity to match the industrial growth of the nation. A prime example is its activity with the Public Service Electric and Gas Company during the enlargement of its fossil fuel generation facilities in the fifteen years following World War II. Most of the generating stations are located in the industrial corridor of northeastern New Jersey in the marshes formed by the confluence of the Hackensack and Passaic rivers, notorious for poor subsoil conditions. The firm was consultant to PSE&G during expansion of the Sewaren, Kearny, and Linden plants and during construction of new plants in Hudson and Bergen counties, as well as in Mercer County on the Delaware River. Foundation investigations were performed for all these facilities leading to recommendations for appropriate foundations for the heavy and sensitive turbines and ancillary structures.

Waste Disposal and Pollution Control

In the field of pollution control, the firm has performed subsurface investigations and foundation designs for more than 50 sewage systems and wastewater treatment plants during the past decade. It has also provided similar services for large industrial plants and other facilities that have had waste disposal problems and problems with containment and treatment of hazardous wastes.

The sewage treatment plant at Yonkers, New York, designed by Greeley and Hansen for the Westchester County Department of Public Works, was completed in 1957. Since available land was scarce, the plant was to be located on fill in the Hudson River outboard of the New York Central Railroad tracks. The firm investigated the subsoils, made design studies and recommendations, and provided inspection during the site filling and foundation construction, under the immediate direction of Stanley J. Johnson. It also conducted laboratory tests and provided design studies for alternative methods of construction. The firm's contract included the design and construction inspection of a sludge loading dock and supplemental facilities.

These activities resulted in development of a filled site with a confining dike, faced with small stone and riprap on the riverside, as the most economical alternative. The subsoil disclosed consisted of soft organic silts and clays overlying compact sand and gravel or bedrock. Since stability analyses demonstrated that the soft river deposits could not support the required fill, a shear key trench was excavated to firm underlying materials lying from 50 to 80 feet beneath the dike.

The firm's experience in soil stabilization during past operations was a great advantage. Vertical sand drains were designed for the inboard fill to reduce settlements where organic silt was not excavated. Later borings confirmed the fact that there would be no future settlement problems where silt had not been removed.

The effective use of fills has played a part, historically, in a number of major waste treatment plants. In Cincinnati, Ohio, for example, the firm pioneered in designing a site made from refuse fills for the expansion of the Mill Creek Wastewater Treatment Plant. By engineering diked lagoons, avoiding the use of piles for the structure, and eliminating the necessity of importing borrow, the firm minimized inconvenience to the community using the facilities and saved the taxpayers millions of dollars.

Another innovative approach to water treatment that improved efficiency and economy was used in the design of the filtration building for the Jerome D. Van DeWater Raw Water Treatment Plant on the Niagara River near Buffalo. Here, a system of vertical anchors was devised and installed to prevent flotation of the 20,000-square-foot structure which, with its floor slab 25 feet below groundwater, was subjected to unusually high hydrostatic pressure. The firm also was consultant on the design of a 1,600-foot intake tunnel running through rock under the Niagara River and emerging in the middle of the stream where extremely strong currents exist. This job included one of the first cases in the United States of mining a horseshoe-shaped cross section by a special tunnel-boring machine.

At the Scott Paper Company site in upper Mobile Bay, Alabama, working with Hazen and Sawyer, the firm designed a 14-foot-high hydraulic fill dike to enclose a waste treatment pond, which was located in a swamp area. The dike, 6,000 feet long, overlies as much as 30 feet of organic silt and will settle as much as 4 feet.

For the recently completed Newark Bay Pumping Station, a $300 million secondary plant, the firm was consultant on all foundations. The underlying Hackensack Meadows and glacial lake deposits varied substantially over the 127-acre site. A program of load testing piles and rock tiedowns resulted in a variety of foundation solutions for the many structures.

Many of the firm's most challenging assignments have been those for clients who have encountered foundation problems during construction.

Construction of the foundation slab of the filtration building at the Van DeWater treatment plant in upstate New York, showing vertical anchors installed into rock to resist uplift and reinforcing steel being set prior to concrete placement.

One such problem was faced by a contractor constructing a new pumping station for the Jamaica Water Pollution Project in Queens, New York, in 1974, where caisson sinking was holding up the entire job.

Called in to remedy the situation, the firm reviewed available soil data, reports on the problems, and its own extensive experience with caisson construction and came to the conclusion that modifications to the caissons were necessary. The cutting edges were much higher than the interior partitions, the slope of the cutting edge too flat, the headroom insufficient, and the reach from wall face to cutting edge base too great for effective operations. When the firm's recommendations were followed, the contractor was able to complete the job without significant delays.

Landfilling at Battery Park City along the Hudson River in the lower west side of Manhattan has created a 100-acre, man-made site of very high commercial value.

CHAPTER 9

URBAN AND SITE DEVELOPMENT

"The job of founding the 'World of Tomorrow' on an ash dump provided a notable opportunity for the young science of soil mechanics to demonstrate its practical aspects."

                        Civil Engineering
                        October 1940

"The area was as strewn with boulders and rubble as the path of a former glacier."[1]

    That was a comment in 1922 describing the proposed site of Yankee Stadium in the Bronx. Borings by the firm (then Moran, Maurice & Proctor) revealed that in the main grandstand area behind home plate there existed a thick deposit of peat over which had been dumped a jumbled layer of rocks from subway excavations. Toward the outfield and in the bleachers area, bedrock was shallow. One solution that seemed feasible to avoid differential settlement was to go to bedrock. However, the cost of this approach appeared to exceed the intended budget for the job. The firm's engineers had encountered similar problems while investigating building sites in lower Manhattan. It was common to find sites filled with debris from subway excavations and building demolition. The solution decided upon was neither new nor unique, but the application was unprecedented. Through the use of slush grout, the boulder deposits were converted into what amounted to a massive foundation mat.

    Atop this, concrete slabs were cast in a radial design, capable of supporting reinforced concrete girders, each fifteen feet deep. Set into the concrete slabs and insulated from them by heavy building paper, these girders in turn supported the columns for the stadium itself.

Initially, it was intended that a framework would be devised at the base of the girders so that hydraulic jacks could be inserted for periodic compensation as the mat settled. During the course of experimentation with this form of jacking, two interesting facts came to light. The first was that the columns were too massive to raise in a single lift without exceeding safe limits. The second was that this jacking action accelerated consolidation of the mat, even when it did not raise any girders. Through the simple alternative of repeated use of the jacks, full consolidation was readily obtained.

Yankee Stadium was not the firm's earliest experience with transforming large areas of unstable material into useful sites for a variety of major installations and purposes. But it typifies one important aspect of the more than 2,000 geotechnical investigations conducted by the firm. Projects have ranged from embankment shoulders for highways to the conversion of swamps to industrial park sites almost 600 acres in size.

The 1939 New York World's Fair

The firm played many roles in this major enterprise during the middle and late thirties, ranging from the overall site investigation to design of foundations for buildings and exhibits, bridges and roads, and tidal gates and dams for the fairground's lakes and waterways.

Flushing Meadow, the 1,200-acre site for the 1939 New York World's Fair, was considered to be little but wasteland at the time of selection, a tidal marsh situated barely a foot above mean high tide. It had been used largely as an ash dump. Initial investigations showed the soil to be composed of organic clays and silts resting on sand and gravel that varied from 15 to 80 feet below the surface. The weight of the ash dump had forced the surface of the meadow downward some 30 to 40 feet below its original level.

The initial problem lay in preventing soil deformations that could jeopardize foundation stability and in preserving as much as possible the inherent structure of the underlying clay-silt deposit. The problems were such that the World's Fair site reclamation became one of the earliest uses of landfill of its kind in civil engineering history. This operation was

More than a thousand acres of ash dump and swamp became invisible and forgotten when the 1939 New York World's Fair became the reality shown in this overview. After an exhaustive site investigation, a controlled filling operation spread more than six million cubic yards of cinders over the swampland, to heights compensating for the anticipated consolidation, calculated from the firm's laboratory data.

preceded by one that the firm was actively familiar with: the Oakland approach to the San Francisco Bay Bridge, where deep deposits of unstable organic silts had to be stabilized through special consolidation methods. It was on the Oakland job that the firm first proposed use of the sand drains that Daniel Moran had patented in 1926 — a method of consolidating soft foundation soils as the job progressed, stabilizing them for the future.

The World's Fair job was an early field demonstration of the marked increase in compressibility and the radical decrease in shear strength of remolded organic silt deposits as compared with undisturbed soils. Because the silt remolding was carefully controlled, settlement of filled areas performed almost exactly as predicted.

As Carlton S. Proctor described the World's Fair site in 1937, "The major foundation problem was not so much the provision of adequate support of vertical loads, but the prevention and control of lateral soil movements. Careful soil mechanics laboratory analyses determined the shearing strength of the silts and of the vegetable humus matter overlying the undisturbed areas and the extents to which consolidations would take place under filled areas . . ."[2]

Other projects at the World's Fair included foundations for the Consolidated Edison and other exhibit buildings, a boat basin, tide gate and dam, diversion channels, and consultation for the design of the fair's theme structure, the Trylon and Perisphere. The success of these projects led quite naturally to later assignments of a similar nature, for the New York World's Fair of 1964, when the firm acted as consultant for site improvements and for such structures as the United States Pavilion and the Science Museum.

Special Site Problems

The General Grant Housing Project, completed in 1957, is not one that would strike the casual observer as being innovative or unusual. It is a complex of eight 21-story buildings in New York City, simply designed and with no frills.

What makes this project unique are the foundations. Located on a very difficult marginal site, the buildings were the tallest structures ever to be supported above the Lake Flushing glacial lake formation. The bedrock depth — from 170 to 265 feet below the surface — ruled out the traditional solution of piles to rock for seven of the eight buildings. The overburden soils consisted of a mixed fill atop glacial outwash sand and a deep glacial lake deposit of varved silt and clay, underlain by a comparatively thin layer of bouldery glacial till.

As a consultant on more than 40 New York public housing projects for the previous twenty years, the firm was well aware of the need to adhere to strict construction budgets. To find an economical alternative to bedrock support, analyses of boring samples and settlement studies were conducted. These studies indicated that the buildings could be

Typical foundation mat being constructed for the General Grant Houses in New York City. The solution to supporting such high structures on a glacial lake formation lay in the design of the mat, five feet thick, approximately 250 by 40 feet in area, and positioned 25 feet below grade. Because foundation costs were a major factor in the design of this housing project, use of the mat system made it possible to stay within a reasonable budget and yet assure safe support.

reliably supported on the upper sand bed, despite its nominal thickness and the depth of the glacial lake stratum below. The solution, developed under project manager James D. Parsons, lay in designing foundation mats of reinforced concrete 5 feet thick and situated about 25 feet below grade. This combination resulted in safe support at reasonable cost.

During the midfifties, the firm was engaged by the New York City Housing Authority as consultants on Coney Island Houses, five 14-story buildings to be founded 10 feet below sea level next to the boardwalk, approximately 150 feet from the ocean. The site was underlain by a 25-foot layer of lightly preconsolidated organic clay at a depth of 60 feet below grade. A hotel and apartment buildings, some of which showed

Aerial view of excavation for the foundation mat for a unit of the Coney Island Housing Project for the New York City Housing Authority. Dewatering for the excavation included a recharge system to protect adjacent structures from settlement.

detrimental differential settlements, adjoined the site. As considerable economy would result from elimination of long piles for support, mat foundations were recommended. Tests indicated that groundwater lowering during construction would cause settlement and damage to the adjacent buildings. To prevent this, a recharge system was installed to inject the water pumped from the well point system for the excavation into the ground in front of the adjacent structures.

A monitoring system demonstrated that groundwater drawdown below the sensitive existing buildings was prevented and no additional settlement or damage to these buildings occurred. This project was an early demonstration of the effectiveness of a groundwater recharge system in maintaining hydrostatic uplift on existing foundations to prevent settlement during construction dewatering.

The firm's ventures into urban-site development have not always focused on specific structures or groups of structures. Many have evolved in the overall development of sites in which a range of foundation objectives has to be achieved. An early project was College Point Industrial Park, for which a study under Bob Johnston was completed in 1962 for the Department of City Planning for the City of New York, following a 1953 study for the Flushing Airport Development. The 591-acre site in the Borough of Queens was largely an undeveloped marsh, whose very nature had discouraged would-be developers and whose terrain was considered both hostile and almost valueless. Could it be economically and effectively transformed into an industrial park for light industry? This was the question that the Planning Department had posed. The firm, in a joint venture with architects and drainage and sanitary engineers, studied the region and then recommended that the industrial park include only 415 of the available acres. The original marsh, with its surface barely above normal high tide, and with very compressible organic soils to depths of 80 feet, had been partially filled with incompatible waste materials. These conditions, combined with unstable natural soil and poor drainage, had deterred previous development schemes. Yet, it was judged that certain foundation treatments and procedures, if carefully followed, could transform the area, physically and economically, into the desired industrial park.

The firm's plan called for a coordinated drainage complex of ditches, dikes, tide gates, auxiliary pumping, and a drainage pond for water storage until low tide permitted outflow. Soils excavated from the pond would be used to elevate building sites (providing a total of six million square feet of floor space) to protect them from high water. Among the recommendations for support facilities were recreation areas, a corporate airstrip, commercial service zones, utilities, access roads, and adjacent highways. The plan also detailed the variations in subsoil profiles for each part of the site, suggesting the types of buildings that would, or would not, be feasible at those locations. These varied from reliable soils that were suitable for support of spread footings to less stable soils requiring piles or replacement by engineered compacted fills.

Nature's imperfections take many forms below ground. A frustrating example of what can happen on an attractive-looking site is the campus of the University of South Florida, where new construction was begun in 1958. Located on a large tract of gently rolling terrain several miles north of Tampa, the buildings were modern in design, apparently serene and secure in their semitropical setting. But beneath them, the story was different. Soils at this site consist of a surface layer of fine sand, the upper part of which is in loose condition, overlying strata of sandy silts and clay, below which lies Tampa limestone, a formation of soft, porous rock. Its most detrimental feature is its susceptibility to loss of support if surface drainage is washed into the cavities in its structure. Sinkholes are common and have often been devastating to residences and public buildings alike.

Called in as consultant, the firm first made recommendations about sites in the area that would be the least susceptible to cavity collapse and formation of sinkholes. Then it designed foundations that would not be jeopardized by these continuing changes below the surface. The unstable nature of the Tampa limestone ruled out piles for structure support. Tests showed that, after compaction of the loose surface sands, spread footings could be relied on to provide safe and adequate support for several buildings. Others, however, had to be founded on continuous mats, spanning over incipient sinks, with enough material excavated to balance the building weight so that no additional load would be imposed on the underlying strata.

The firm has provided counsel on many other projects where existing buildings have suffered loss of support because of subsurface weaknesses. Many such cases have involved industrial plants and related facilities, particularly in southeastern portions of the United States where these problems are commonplace. Characteristic programs include drilling and grouting, the control and disposal of surface water, and the prevention of leakages into the ground.

The firm has taken an active role in studying, correcting, and preventing landslides. A major involvement of this type has been in the Pacific Palisades section of Los Angeles, where escarpments rise as much as 300 feet above the sea, with slopes from 10 to more than 60 degrees to the horizontal. Landslides and erosion are natural to these formations.

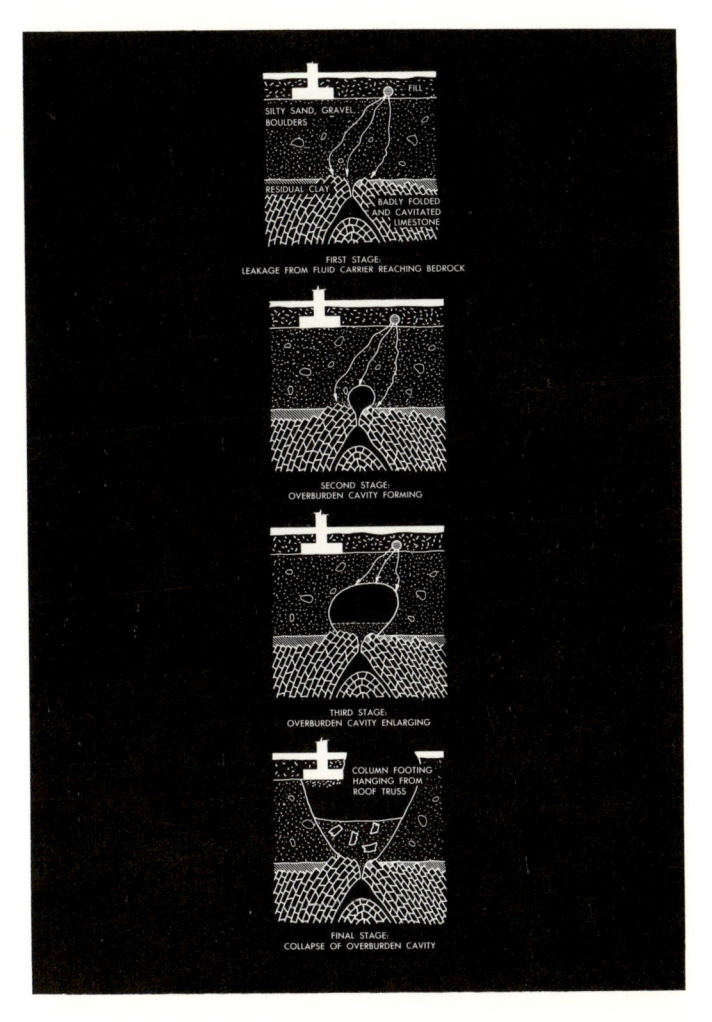

The four diagrams show (top to bottom) the sequence in the development of cavities under a foundation, which eventually leads to failure. The problem is especially characteristic of limestone strata in the southeastern United States, where the firm has conducted numerous studies for clients. The University of Southern Florida case is typical of the problems faced and the solutions recommended.

For a major study, starting in 1958 and ending in 1960, the firm's engineering team mapped and classified more than 100 such slides and intensely investigated 34 of them. The resultant studies included some 9,000 linear feet of test borings, widespread measurement of groundwater levels, and observations of slope movements by inclinometers. Also evaluated were the influence on the region of seismicity, erosion, rainfall, domestic water use, irrigation, and the nearby construction of buildings and highways.

Six major types of slides were isolated and identified, their movements dictated chiefly by groundwater levels, the history of past instability, and the nature of two specific types of tertiary clay strata. As a result, it was possible to recommend a long-range program to prevent and correct the coastal landslide problems.

This escarpment at Pacific Palisades typifies the continuing landslides of varying proportions that occur along the fifteen-mile stretch of California coast between Santa Monica and Latigo Shores in Los Angeles County. The slide shown has completely covered the coastal highway north of Los Angeles. The firm was retained in 1959 to evaluate causes and recommend corrective procedures for these problems.

Reclaiming Marginal Lands for Urban Development

Over the years, the firm has provided guidance in creating more space for urban regions through marginal land development. The Flushing Meadow site was one such example, though for the immediate, limited objective of providing a site for the World's Fair. Equally important are those sites that will form solid additions to a city itself, as in the case of the lower Manhattan areas of New York City.

Philip C. Rutledge described this field of specialization in his Terzaghi Lecture in February 1969, in which he pointed out that many of America's major cities have room for expansion only by developing the swamps, marshes, and other wetlands adjacent to them. There is nothing new, he said, about creating usable land, and one has only to look at old maps of Boston and New York to realize the expansion that has taken place since their foundings.

"What is new," he added, "is the appearance on the scene of the professional planners, a tremendous increase in planning activity, and the sociological and artistic basis for many of the plans."[3]

He defined the problems as fourfold: (1) To make dry land; (2) to make usable land; (3) to provide foundation support for the structures that will be put on the land; and (4) to create a waterfront separation between land and open water.

One of the firm's major examples of such design work is the Battery Park City development, for which it had responsibility for designing 92 acres of new land on the site of abandoned Hudson River piers. The planned multibillion-dollar complex of offices and apartment buildings, shops, park, and recreational facilities forms what is probably the most valuable single real-estate development in the country. Basic responsibilities included the initial site investigations, soil research, and foundation recommendations. The firm also provided engineering services that ranged from design and field inspection of bulkheads to dredging plans, filling procedures, and sand drain consolidation operations. The cost estimate for land construction proved to be accurate within three percent.

In one area of Battery Park City, subsoils were consolidated by installation of jetted sand drains, as shown in the photograph, and use of surcharge up to 25 feet in height. This fill, which was procured from lower New York Harbor by hopper dredge, was placed hydraulically, then compacted with vibrating rollers and sealed off with asphaltic materials to provide working surfaces and prevent the blowing of particles during high wind conditions.

The South Industrial Area of the Long Wharf Redevelopment Project in New Haven, Connecticut, during construction in the early 1960s. The firm's design included some 30,000 sand drains averaging 40 feet in length. Stabilization of the fill enabled use of slab on grade and spread footings and avoided costly measures for support of utilities and pavements.

With a thorough knowledge of local construction capabilities and equipment, the firm segmented the overall land reclamation work to attract a maximum number of qualified contractors. One of the advantages of this reclamation was that, at least initially, it would be highly competitive, offering new land at one-twentieth of the cost of adjacent inland properties. It was significant that the final costs for creating the site were about $1.5 million less than estimated for the original budget of $46 million for direct construction costs.

A similar land reclamation example is the Long Wharf Redevelopment Project in New Haven, Connecticut, for which the firm's team, under the direction of James D. Parsons, prepared a feasibility study and then designed the 120-acre site stabilization.

"This is a classical example of the merit of stabilization," said partner Robert C. Johnston, "where there is sufficient time available for this purpose ... In an operation of this type it is always gratifying when the performance conforms as closely to the design. Settlements of the largest and heaviest building constructed on the site have ranged only about one-half to one inch during the first ten years after the building was completed."[4]

The area consisted of a portion of the New Haven waterfront that had been isolated by the filling for the Connecticut Turnpike and was not then usable. The site was covered by organic clay, soft and compressible, ranging in thickness from 10 to 40 feet. The method used to develop this marginal land was a combination of fill, vertical sand drains, and surcharge.

"Surcharge," said Johnston, "is a simple, direct method to accelerate settlements. The surcharge load is usually additional fill piled to a height to produce a desired extra loading. The magnitude of the load is such that, after a relatively short period of time, the underlying settlement will approximate the same as that caused by surface structures over a period of about 20 years."[5]

This principle has proved effective in an increasing number of cases in hastening the settlement process so that much of it can be accomplished even before final construction gets under way.

The previously mentioned Westside Highway Project included design of a 2,000-foot-long test prototype embankment section extending 500 to 700 feet offshore from the bulkhead line along the Hudson River atop deposits of organic silt up to more than 200 feet in thickness. Environmental restraints required containment of construction-created turbidity, which led to design of a full-depth silt retention curtain anchored to the river bottom. The curtain can accommodate normal tidal fluctuations of 5 feet, with gates for entrance and exit of construction vessels.

A number of stabilizing methods were incorporated in the design of the fill placement, including dredging of a shear key, placement of perimeter rock dikes, time-phased lifts of embankment and surcharge material, and use of various types of sand and wick drains installed under 20 to 30 feet of water. An extensive array of instrumentation was designed to be installed to monitor embankment stability and settlement for control of fill-placement rates and to determine the comparative effectiveness of the various types of vertical drains.

The prototype embankment was to establish the criteria for subsequent designs of embankments for nearly three miles of landfill. Creation of a stable embankment in the river was a key element in this landmark project.

Upgrading the Value and Utility of Upland Sites

Not all land is reclaimed from swamps, dilapidated waterfront acreage, or sanitary landfills. Some valuable properties have been developed from usable, but encumbered upland sites. One example is the Empire State Plaza in Albany, New York, a complex of modern state office buildings constructed in the center of the city. Essentially, the complex is constructed on a 20-acre concrete platform with five underground levels,

Foundation construction for the Empire State Plaza in Albany, New York, in 1967 followed the demolition of low-rise structures and terraced and braced excavations to prevent slope movements in the sensitive Albany Clay.

a network of utility tunnels, and a connecting tunnel to the capitol. The firm was responsible for the site investigation and foundation planning and design and also furnished a resident inspection staff during the foundation construction, to supplement the state's supervisory and inspection teams.

Since excavation for the basements of buildings and the lowest floor of the parking structure was as much as 70 feet below grade and 40 feet below groundwater level, the firm designed construction procedures requiring benched excavations with inclined rakers for excavation support to maintain stable excavation slopes for all stages of construction. The procedures successfully prevented lateral movements of the varved clay during excavation, pile driving, and concrete placement.

A major innovation was the demonstration of the suitability of steel-bearing piles stressed to 12,000 psi instead of the 9,000 psi that had formerly been allowed, with considerable cost savings.

Dredge Spoil Studies

Disposal of waterways dredge spoil in the New York area has been severely restricted by environmental regulations. Mueser Rutledge Consulting Engineers, collaborating with Malcolm Pirnie, Inc., is performing feasibility studies for the New York District Corps of Engineers on the use of dredge spoil as daily and final cover at sanitary landfill sites. River-bottom sediments have been sampled at 30 locations within the Greater New York Harbor and tested for physical properties. Investigations of upland disposal sites for the dredge spoil have also been conducted. Schematic designs for dewatering the wet dredged material, time estimates for dewatering, and leachate collection systems were developed by the firm for this new project.

Ten years after construction had begun, Empire State Plaza was a complex of modern government and public buildings rising from a twenty-acre concrete foundation designed by the firm.

144

The massive concrete slab and heavy piers used to support the silos of the Lone Star Cement Corporation in Hudson, New York, can clearly be identified during this stage of construction. After completing its site investigation and making numerous borings and tests of underlying soils that proved to be unstable, the firm recommended the pier-and-slab design for facilities requiring the handling of heavy loads.

CHAPTER 10

INDUSTRIAL DEVELOPMENTS

"The business of building is not new. Man has been erecting structures to overcome natural obstacles for over 1,000 years. What distinguishes current efforts from those of the ancients is efficiency."

Golden Jubilee Annual, 1975
Construction Division, ASCE

The firm had barely entered its founding year in 1910 when it began accepting foundation consulting assignments for large industrial clients. Among those turning to the firm for engineering prior to the 1920s were the International Cement Corporation, American Sugar Refining, Union Bag and Paper Company, Johns-Manville, Ford Motor Company, and Bethlehem Steel. They would be joined later by companies manufacturing a wide range of products, from foods and chemicals to plastics, electronics, petroleum, metals, pharmaceuticals, building supplies, and communications equipment.

It was appropriate, in view of its own close involvement with the product, that the firm should undertake numerous assignments for the cement industry, as well as for others in the field of construction materials. An early and longtime client was the Lone Star Cement Company, for which it designed foundations for distribution terminals, manufacturing plants, and storage silos. A characteristic example was the foundation design for cement silos in Hudson, New York, completed in 1940. These structures are excellent illustrations of the kinds of foundation problems encountered when heavy storage facilities are sited in locations with generally weak or unstable soils. Site investigation and soil analyses require meticulous attention to produce effective designs.

At the Hudson site, borings revealed some 50 feet of clay and loose granular material and copious groundwater. The final decision was to build 48 piers inside individual steel-sheeted cofferdams driven to bedrock. These supported a heavy concrete slab, which in turn supported 27 individual storage bins. Holding the number of piers to a minimum provided necessary space for installation of cement-handling equipment in a basement under the main silo support slab. This was but one of a variety of foundations that were designed for cement companies in locations ranging throughout North and South America.

At a cement plant in Parana, Argentina, a completely different type of problem emerged during one of the firm's earlier consulting assignments in 1939. Shortly before its completion, the San Martin

Retained to recommend a solution to the foundation problems at San Martin, the firm designed underpinning and pile replacement. As shown here, replacement piles were jacked into position without appreciable interruption of the plant's operations.

Foundation piles at the San Martin Cement Plant in Parana, Argentina, which were damaged during driving because of boulders in the underlying fill.

Carlton S. Proctor inspecting the repair work at the San Martin Cement Plant in Parana, Argentina.

Cement Plant suffered a large-scale earth slide that threatened the safety of a number of structures. A broad portion of the plant site, as well as the hillside behind it, was underlain by sloping layers of sand and clay, which had been protected by impervious materials. Some years earlier, however, the uphill cover had been stripped in the course of quarrying limestone for the cement plant. Rainwater had infiltrated the exposed sediments, causing slides along the slippery surfaces of the sloping clay

The unique sloping floor of the gas holder for the Southern California Gas Company is clearly visible in this photograph taken as the foundation neared completion in 1941. The challenge faced by the firm was to design a facility with maximum capacity, within height limits imposed by Los Angeles building codes.

stratum. The installation of an intercepting trench with perforated drainpipes, sheet-pile cutoff wall, and concrete gutters at the surface was successful in preventing further slides.

The firm was also retained to make a study of distressed storage and powerhouse foundations on that site. A search of local construction records revealed two things: first, that borings made prior to construction had not disclosed that half of the plant would rest on 75 feet of fill, nearly a century old, that had been dumped at the site from adjacent quarrying operations; and second, that the precast concrete piles had stopped at shallow penetrations, resting in the middle of the boulder-strewn fill instead of on what the builders assumed was firm support. Loads from the new fill and the plant structures had caused compression, sliding, and severe settlements. None of the piles had penetrated the fill. Many had hit boulders that twisted or shattered them so they provided little or no support.

Without interrupting plant operations, the firm's engineers directed the excavation of underpinning trenches deep enough to expose two rows of piles under the structure, then gradually expanded them laterally. The solution was twofold: extending the intact precast piles by plumb posting and forcing them down by hydraulic jacks until compact sand beneath the fill was reached; and replacing the damaged piles with open-ended pipe piles, also jacked to the underlying sand stratum.

A Range of Industrial Solutions

The ten-million-cubic-foot water-seal gas holder, completed in 1941 in Los Angeles for the Southern California Gas Company, is one of many such foundations on which the firm built an early reputation. A design problem was created by local building regulations limiting the height of the structure. To obtain maximum capacity within the permissible height, the entire water-sealing structure was placed below grade. To reduce costs, only the perimeter of the interior was excavated to the necessary depth. The interior floor, paved to make it watertight, was designed so that it sloped upward toward the center.

The White Pine Copper Company development in Michigan imposed a number of challenging problems, including two concrete arch tunnels to the copper mine, smelter and storage-bin underpinning, and foundations for a heavy 500-foot reinforced-concrete gas discharge stack. The site for the stack posed real problems. The soil profile comprised 50 feet of red, sandy, silty clay containing some gravel and cobbles underlain by boulders, gravel, and broken rock. Bedrock was at a depth of 65 feet. The red, silty clay had unusual characteristics: high compressibility and relatively low shear strength, despite high density. This combination of characteristics was attributed to the calcium carbonate content or the presence of nontronite, an uncommon clay mineral. The boulders and unbroken rock made it impractical to consider

This 500-foot reinforced concrete discharge stack at the White Pine Copper Company in northwestern Michigan was sited over a loose mixture of sand, clay, gravel, cobbles, and fractured rock. The firm's solution was to avoid load concentration, utilizing an 85-foot-wide octagonal stepped mat of reinforced concrete that supported the stack with minimal settlement.

any type of pile foundation to rock. The solution: an octagonal mat foundation of reinforced concrete, 85 feet across and stepped in thickness from 6 to 13 feet. Despite the thick bed of low-bearing-capacity soil, the settlement was less than one inch.

Completely different in nature was the foundation plan for a Goodyear synthetic rubber plant completed in Beaumont, Texas, in 1960. Called in to investigate the site and develop foundation design procedures, the firm encountered clayey subsoils that were highly plastic and subject to wide seasonal variations in moisture content above the water table. These conditions resulted in alternate shrinkage and swelling of the clay and would subject shallow foundations to excessive movements.

The firm was retained by the White Pine Copper Company to design two cut-and-cover concrete arch tunnel approaches to the company's mine, each 800 feet long. Construction of the tunnel utilized the unusual traveling form shown above.

The firm undertook extensive subsurface investigations and developed alternative foundation designs, construction procedures, and cost estimates. These studies dictated that structures not be built on near-surface soils. However, it was determined that lightly loaded foundations — typical of much of the plant's layout — could be supported safely by excavating no more than six feet of the surface materials and replacing them with compacted sand backfill. The more heavily loaded structures were supported by drilled and belled piers, while the tall towers used in the manufacture of isoprene were supported on deep mat foundations.

During the 1950s, the firm was called in by a number of aluminum producers to assist in expanding existing sites and locating new sites to accommodate the country's need for expanded production facilities. For the Kaiser Aluminum and Chemical Corporation, alternative properties were evaluated along the lower Mississippi and a site at Gramercy, Louisiana, was selected for construction of a new reduction plant. The assignment continued at the selected site with preparation of foundation recommendations for the plant structures and dock facilities. When Kaiser decided to expand its facilities in Jamaica, West Indies, to include a new plant to produce aluminum at the bauxite source rather than shipping the bauxite to the States for reduction, it selected the firm to perform a geologic reconnaissance of four sites including seismic exploration and confirmatory borings. Site preparation specifications were developed for the selected plant construction including methods of excavation, crushing, and rolling the native limestone into a stable fill for plant structure support.

Aluminium Laboratories, Ltd., of Montreal retained the firm to review five upstate New York sites for construction of a new hot rolling mill. Following a comparison of factors, including detailed site preparation costs developed during the evaluation, a site in Oswego was selected. The firm prepared recommendations for the site preparation and foundation design to accommodate the glacial till and boulder strata overlying variable rock features for the 350,000-square-foot structure.

Serving the Nuclear Industry

Improving the safety of nuclear plants through reliable foundation planning has been on the firm's agenda almost since this form of energy was first commercially developed. Starting with assignments at the earlier-described Savannah River Plant and a nuclear power station in Italy in the early 1950s, the firm undertook such assignments as consultants for the Atomic Energy Commission's "Project Plowshare" in 1959, the study of a new Panama Canal excavated by controlled nuclear explosives, and foundations for the Bevatron in Berkeley, California. In the latter case, the sensitivity of the facilities called for total integrity of the foundations, with extremely limited tolerance for settlements.

Important design elements were contributed by the firm for the underpinning of the Auxiliary Building and Service Water Pump Structure at the Consumers Power Company's Midland, Michigan, Nuclear Power Plant. The work, adjacent to twin nuclear reactors, was a most difficult and sensitive underpinning project. The firm provided the plant designer/constructor, the Bechtel Power Corporation, with extensive consultation, design, and inspection services, and established stringent control for the settlement of the structures during the foundation installations. Besides pit underpinning, the job included placement of a partial wall foundation beneath the reactors' auxiliary building, the improvement of construction schedules and preparation of a major alternative design. The underpinning project was one of the largest and most elaborately engineered that had ever been undertaken.

Other industrial jobs and ventures have ranged from investigations into the collapse of underground storage tanks to settlement above mine workings, laying pipelines, stability investigations of towers and retaining walls, evaluating fire damage, correcting excessive vibration in factories, flood protection, assessing heat damage to foundations, and neutralizing corrosion damage to piles caused by saltwater or chemicals.

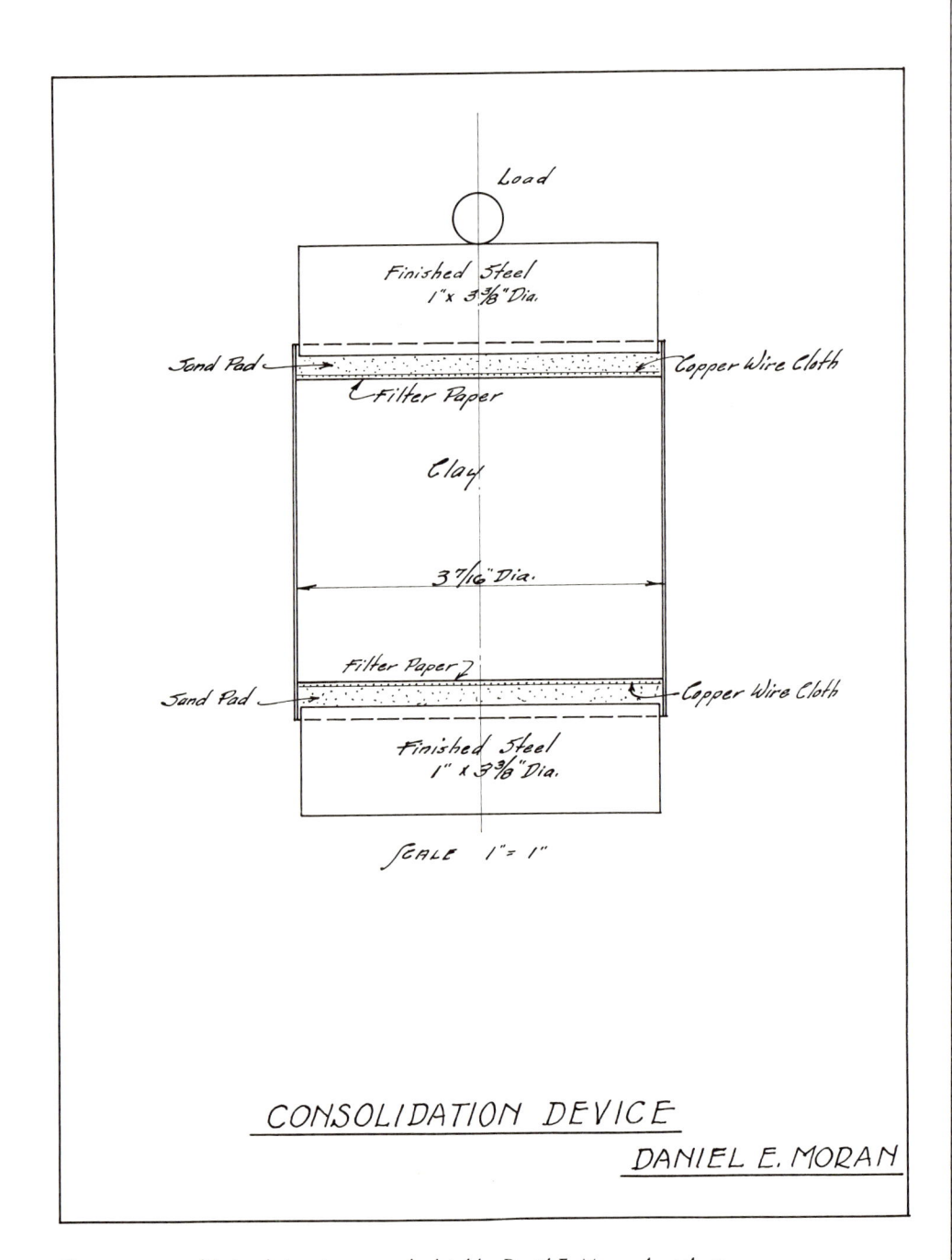

Floating ring consolidation device, circa 1910, developed by Daniel E. Moran about the time he was establishing his new foundation firm. Moran was a pioneer in the study of the property of soils and was among the first to understand the nature of volume change in clay and silt soils under loads and apply this knowledge to actual foundation problems.

CHAPTER 11

RESEARCH, FIELD INVESTIGATIONS, AND TESTING

"In the early 1920s, there began a concerted scientific effort to determine the physical laws responsible for the behavior of the subsurface materials from which foundations derive their support. The new field of endeavor, known as soil mechanics, . . . has provided new techniques for selecting the appropriate types of foundation under a given set of conditions and for predicting the performance of the completed substructure."

Foundation Engineering
John Wiley & Sons, 1953

Historical references of many kinds indicate that foundation engineering had its origins in antiquity and enabled ancient peoples to construct enormous monuments and public works that survived intact for centuries. It is all the more astonishing, therefore, that trial and error and accumulated experience played a far greater part in foundation design and construction than did any scientific discipline. The guiding spirit of modern soil mechanics was the late Karl Terzaghi, who was probably the first engineer to undertake comprehensive investigations of the properties of soils shortly after the beginning of the twentieth century.

He was closely followed in this field by Daniel E. Moran, who possessed such an innate curiosity about the structure and content of the world around him that his efforts at research were inevitable.

As early as 1910, Moran's interest in soil mechanics led him to experiment with consolidation testing of "undisturbed" samples of clay and other materials. In Moran's early consolidation device, a thin-walled brass cylinder served as a sampling instrument as well as the sample container during testing. His invention utilized two pistons and a test cylinder that was supported by the friction of the soil sample on the cylinder walls (floating ring consolidometer). Sometimes, however, the pistons would tilt and jam in the cylinder.

An improvement was developed by the firm in the early 1930s, prompted by the need for the laboratory testing of clay samples during foundation work on the San Francisco-Oakland Bay Bridge. A guiding mechanism was perfected that effectively prevented the pistons from jamming. A further improvement was the addition of a heavy spring, which maintained load on the soil sample and overcame the problem of load reduction caused by compression of the sample. The resulting device was further modified so that it could test samples in two different diameters: 4⅞ and 2½ inches.

During the Bay Bridge operations, the soil tests were conducted at the University of California laboratory and the firm's own laboratory on both undisturbed and remolded samples. Tests were also performed to determine the effects of boundary pore pressure on the consolidation process.

Field Investigations and Laboratory Soil Tests

Although by no means confined to the investigation of sites and solutions to foundation problems, the firm's operations in the areas of research and testing have helped over the years to develop foundation and geotechnical engineering from an art into a science. The firm was the first one in private practice in the United States to establish a soils laboratory. In a sense, this field of activity goes back almost three-quarters of a century to those rudimentary tests made by Moran to help him understand the behavior of soils and their reactions to pressure. His studies stimulated future investigations.

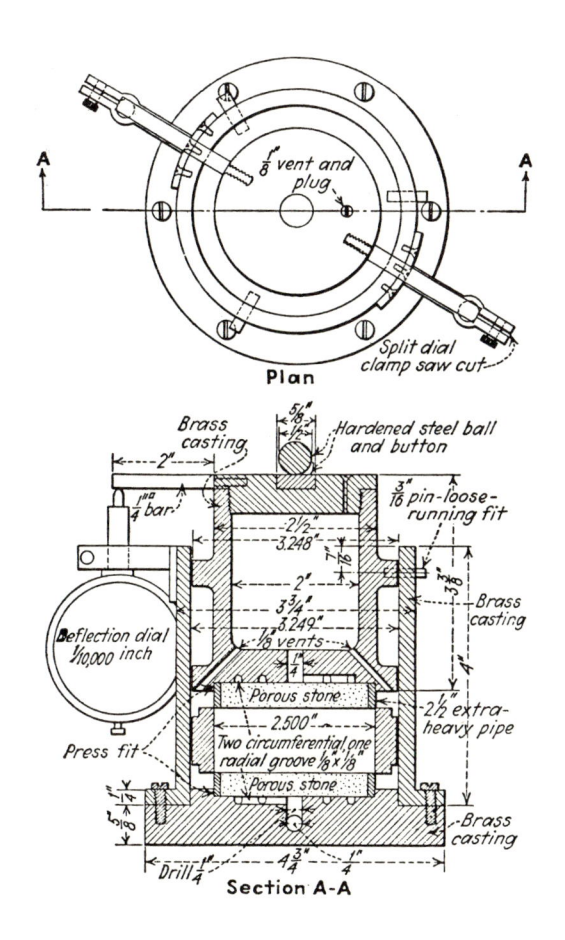

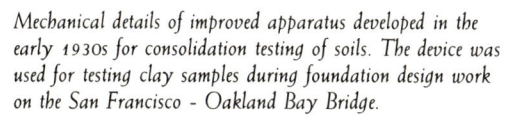

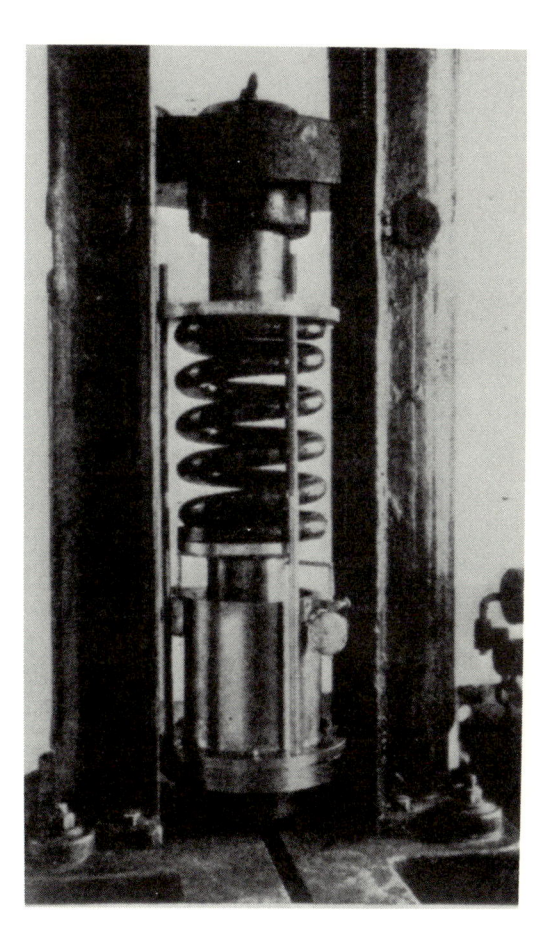

Mechanical details of improved apparatus developed in the early 1930s for consolidation testing of soils. The device was used for testing clay samples during foundation design work on the San Francisco - Oakland Bay Bridge.

Improved consolidation test apparatus in position in testing machine.

During the early 1930s, both at the Bay Bridge site and elsewhere, soil samples were taken in many places by inserting special tube samplers through previously sunk drill casing, and forcing them into the underlying materials. Once in the laboratory, only the soil at the center of the cylinder was tested, under the assumption that the soil at the ends and sides would have been disturbed or softened by the distortions in sampling. Moran later observed that the computation was often affected by the presence of swelling and that this was caused by minute pockets of gas in the soil — gas which expanded after it was brought to the surface from the depths. Through experimentation, he and his partners perfected testing devices that attempted to allow for these distorting factors.

In the mid-1930s, the sampling device that had been used for the San Francisco-Oakland Bay Bridge was further modified and improved, this time for the firm's work on the 1939 World's Fair site. Known as the

Testing box devised by Moran in 1924 to determine and demonstrate stress distribution beneath a rectangular footing. The bin, four feet square by three feet deep, was filled with layers of sand and compacted by ramming. Since the layers of sand were separated by layers of white powder, the effect of compression could be observed through the plate-glass front of the bin as increasing loads were applied.

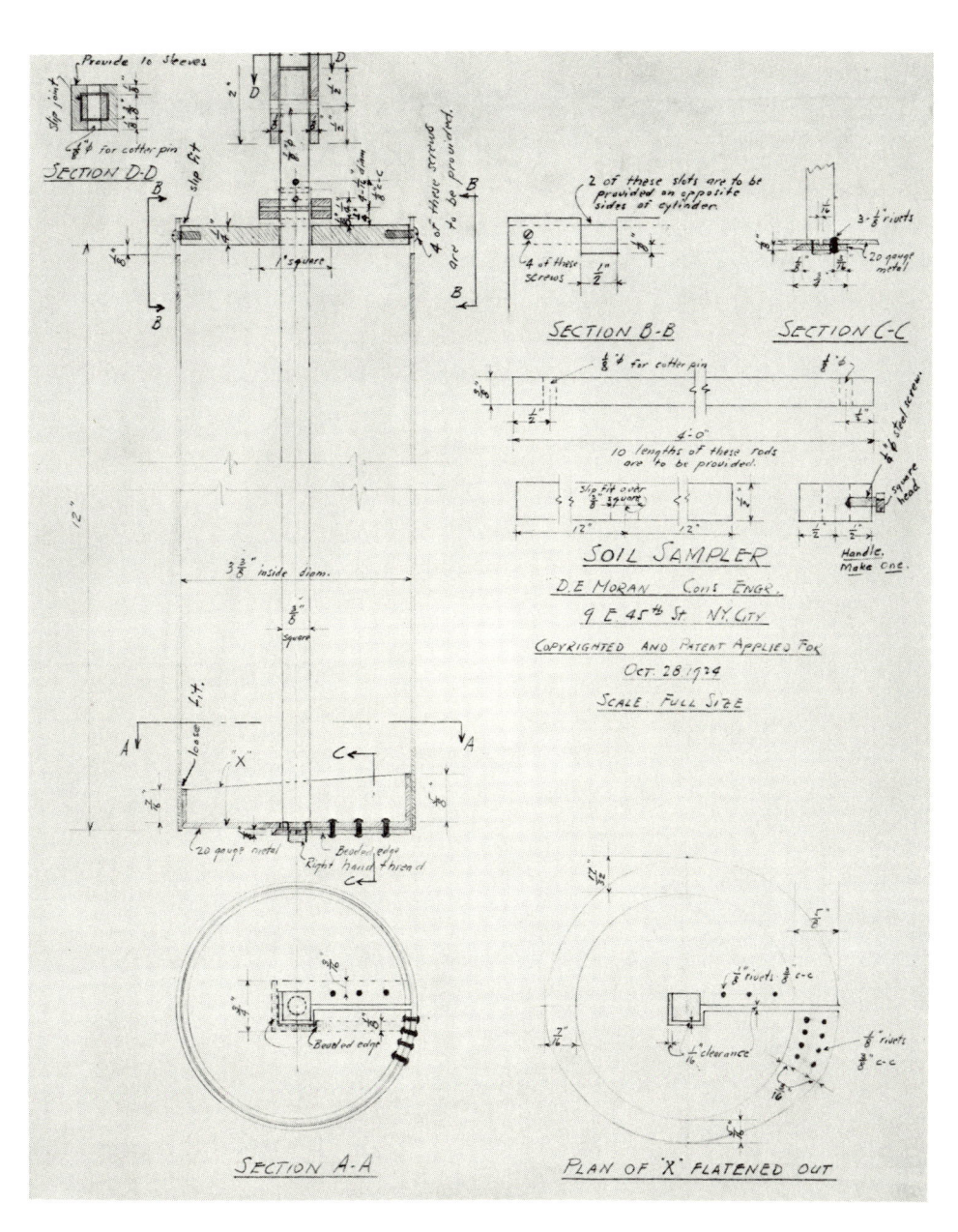

In 1924, Moran developed this device for taking undisturbed samples of soil. Through his early years of testing subsurface materials at various foundation sites, he had realized that erroneous data often resulted from tests because the samples were disturbed during sampling. This sampler and his recommended method of obtaining samples led to more representative test results.

Moran and Proctor sampler, it had a three-inch-diameter brass liner and a split barrel to ease removal of samples.

Much of the testing for the World's Fair site, as well as for the firm's work with tunnel borings under the Hudson River, was undertaken with the help of Professor Donald M. Burmeister who had developed a pilot laboratory at Columbia University for this kind of investigation.

One of the fundamental problems was not only that of the testing procedures and methods, but the fact that communication was difficult. The implications were often misunderstood. "The existing confusion in soil classification standards," wrote partner Carlton S. Proctor at the time, "is largely a confusion in terminology, and a standard classification is to be expected only after the establishment of a standard terminology. The first step in this direction should be agreement as to the number of classifications to apply to each soil group."[1]

At the end of the 1930s, however, recognizing that these standards would be developed in time, the firm started to install equipment and perfect a practical laboratory that could test all kinds of samples sent in from the field from a wide range of sources. William Kimball and Hamilton Gray further developed a laboratory that was in part-time use in the firm prior to 1936. When James D. Parsons joined the firm in 1940, one of his responsibilities was to develop the soil laboratory. He was well qualified to do so, having served for three years at the Harvard Graduate School of Engineering as Research Assistant in Soil Mechanics. Under his guidance, the soil laboratory rapidly grew in capability, acquiring equipment for measuring properties related to consolidation, permeability, compression, shear resistance, and plasticity.

In the 1940s, Parsons made successful use of a simple clean-out jet auger with calyx, which was manufactured to an MPF&M design by Sprague & Henwood. The device facilitated removal of cuttings and disturbed material from the borehole just above the material to be taken as samples, prior to use of an undisturbed sampling device. The drilling fluid was deflected horizontally, thus minimizing disturbance of the underlying soil. (The firm still requires use of the clean-out auger prior to use of an undisturbed sampler.)

161

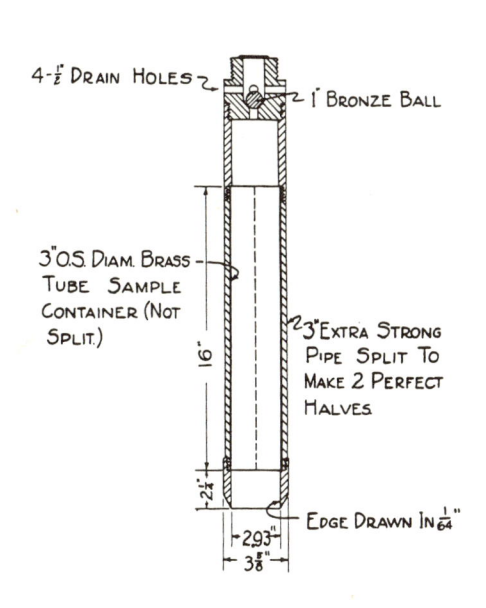

Device For Taking Undisturbed Soil Samples

The first drive sampler with a liner used in the United States was developed for the San Francisco - Oakland Bay Bridge project according to instructions from the firm. Shown here is an improved sampler designed by Moran & Proctor in the mid-1930s for investigating the site of the 1939 New York World's Fair at Flushing Meadow.

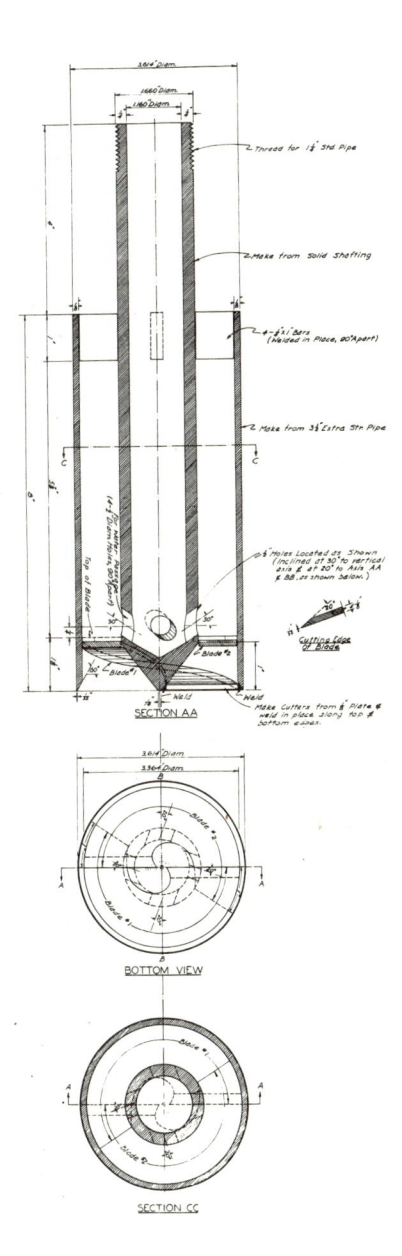

In the 1940s, the firm designed a clean-out jet auger and had units manufactured to its own specifications. This device made it possible to remove materials from test boreholes while minimizing disturbance in preparation for sampling.

Among the jobs that benefited from the development of the soil laboratory during the years it was being developed were Idlewild (now JFK) and La Guardia Airports in New York, whose sites required extensive investigation; the Navy dry dock in Bayonne, New Jersey, which had complex pumping requirements; and many of the early buildings for the New York City Housing Authority, which were positioned on sites where the postglacial lake deposits were deep.

In 1949, Robert C. Hong began work on a new piston sampler for the recovery of undisturbed samples. His system utilized a special drive shoe for the casing, which permitted seating of the piston cylinder. The sampling tube was activated by a ratchet bar with a coupling to the drill rods. The system eliminated the need for the cumbersome "spaghetti rods" which are standard for fixed-piston samples. The sample tube could be activated by a pulley system. The special drive shoe head prevented overwashing with the clean-out auger and kept the piston sampler from exerting downward pressure on the soil being sampled. Although Hong's device became obsolete with the advent of the hydraulic fixed-piston sampler, it represented one more step in the development of the science of soil mechanics.

The arrival of Philip C. Rutledge as a partner in 1952 did much to continue the firm's commitment to the scientific testing of soils during all phases of site and foundation investigations. As one of the country's outstanding soil engineers, he had served for ten years as a professor of civil engineering and department chairman at Northwestern University. It was under his direction, during the 1950s, that soil testing took on a much more significant role. Today, the firm maintains readily accessible files of soil properties and observed performance criteria that have evolved from the many years of operation of the laboratory. These data have been invaluable in making engineering judgments, particularly in cases where there is a lack of contemporary site information.

Rutledge summed up the firm's evaluations for site development and land reclamation in his 1969 Terzaghi Lecture. He discussed some of the limitations of analyses and causes of settlements, such as the consolidation of soils, shear deformations, groundwater effects, and the densification caused by stress increases or vibration. All of these, he said, were "susceptible to analysis by soil mechanics methods." Other causes, however, such as loss of structural capacity of foundation elements or the disturbance of soils because of adjacent construction operations, "are foundation engineering problems where experience and judgment are needed to the maximum degree."

He was careful to point out that, although laboratory tests were of great value, results had to be tempered by a realization of the limitations. He singled out two in particular: the fact that "soils are the product of nature and do not have the homogeneity and uniformity of man-made products," and hence do not fit easily into neat categories; and the fact that even the most extensive borings at a site provide "only one part in 60,000 of the soils affecting a foundation." Emphasizing what Daniel E. Moran had discovered some 60 years earlier, he reminded readers that "the sample has been subjected to some degree of disturbance by the actions of securing it in a sampling device, removing it from the ground and transferring it into a laboratory testing device."

In conclusion, he said, as spokesman for his firm's stand on investigation and testing, "Soil mechanics has come a long way in providing tools to make estimates that are highly useful to the foundation engineer. Most of the real progress has come from case histories where field observations on full-scale structures are combined with thorough subsurface exploration and high-quality laboratory testing."[2]

The World Financial Center rises from made land riverward of the World Trade Center at Battery Park City in lower Manhattan.

CHAPTER 12

CONCLUSION

"In the late 60s, with a landfill operation under way to create 90 acres along the Hudson River, New York City unveiled a billion-dollar scheme for a riverside community, touted as the biggest undertaking since Rockefeller Center. Now, having weathered two recessions and many snags that delayed it for more than a decade, the Battery Park City project has a strong foothold on the sandy strip."

>   Engineering News-Record
>   *April 14, 1983*

For some fifteen years, the subject of Battery Park City had been on the minds of several dozen engineering firms, real-estate developers, government agencies, industrial leaders, and private citizens in the United States and Canada. A longtime dream, it is now an ongoing reality, involving billions of dollars, millions of man-hours, and untold professional skills.

Like every such megajob dependent upon the reclamation and use of land, the first efforts of Battery Park City started, in the late 1960s, at the bottom. In this case, the bottom was unusually complicated. Mueser Rutledge reported in an April 1983 *Engineering News-Record* cover story on the World Financial Center, "the site has three different soil conditions. Under the 41-story southernmost building, called Building A, there is up to 45 feet of 'miscellaneous debris' from the World Trade Center excavation contained by a cellular cofferdam. To the north, there is sand fill under the tower portion of the 45-story Building B. There are also two existing sand-covered relieving platforms over river water and the PATH [subway] tubes in the river bottom. . . . Farther north, the 52-story Building C and the 35-story Building D sit on surcharged sand fill."

All four buildings have combinations of caisson and/or pile foundations, which extend as deep as 70 feet, anchored in bedrock. An immediate problem was that the basement walls on one side of all three buildings abutted the site of Westway, the proposed new highway that had itself been many years in the planning. This eventuality precluded using soil outside the walls to resist lateral wind loads, because the construction of Westway would necessitate removing the soil and leave the buildings unsupported laterally. As a result, Mueser Rutledge devised an alternative of battered caissons in the building cores to resist all lateral loads.

Buildings B and D posed different sets of foundation problems. Building D's 62-foot-deep basement, as well as Building B's 50-foot-deep basement, required permanent slurry walls to contain the full river-water head and soil pressures. Other challenges in designing the basements included the need for high-capacity anchors to resist these pressures. With the Hudson River flowing alongside the landfill site, and with the integrity of the foundations dependent upon so many countermeasures to resist water and soil pressures as well as building loads, the project was — and continues to be — a fine example of the many challenges that face foundation engineers.

It is fitting to conclude with this brief case history of Battery Park City for it graphically pinpoints the very specialized nature of the firm's work on a project where the engineering complexities are so obvious and where teamwork is so essential. Like the proverbial iceberg, most of the foundation design lies below, completely out of sight, and even nonexistent in the mind of the nonprofessional observer. Professionals who are committed to the field of foundation engineering maintain what is described in public relations parlance as a "low profile," generally conservative by nature, though often innovative and creative in their solutions to tough technical and technological problems. Such is the collective commitment of the partners of Mueser Rutledge Consulting Engineers, who have elected to specialize in this field.

To accomplish the firm's objective, the early partners decided that their professional services would be limited to fields of practice consistent with foundation engineering, soils, waterfront construction, and special or difficult structural problems, and not expand to broad engineering services as many consulting firms have done. By staying within these bounds, the staff was able to develop through regular participation in design and fieldwork, a necessity since the practical applications of true foundation engineering are seldom available in texts or through traditional engineering courses.

Many of the staff members have been with the firm for more than 25 years, sharpening their expertise in practical, economic designs and construction procedures. This is implemented by using the firm's storehouse of 75 years of experience and record-keeping, utilizing engineers with long foundation experience, both for office design and field inspection. Most importantly, all work is closely and directly supervised by at least one partner.

The firm has prospered and has been successful in maintaining its size of approximately 100 people regardless of changes in the economy. An employee-to-partner ratio of roughly twenty to one assures sufficient personal involvement by a partner in each engineering assignment to attain the quality of work on which the firm has built its reputation.

Senior staff and supervisory personnel have usually been developed from within the organization. The firm's reputation has been fostered by its considerable experience and expertise in solving specialized problems. Its skills are maintained through internal strengths generated by a stable professional staff. Since the majority of the senior people in the office have spent most of their professional careers with the firm, it is apparent that this philosophy has been reasonably successful.

Because the practice has been purposely limited to foundation work and related fields, and because the partners and staff have committed themselves to this specialized service, the firm is in a prime position to keep abreast of new technological developments and the growing body of theoretical concepts. Equally important, the firm has met numerous challenges by developing new methods, procedures, and equipment. Examples of this kind of innovation have been the sand-drain soil consolidation technique; air locks for pneumatic work; deep bridge caissons; floating wharves; sand-island caisson construction; special grouting and stabilization procedures; specialized bracing for deep foundations; and innovative underpinning methods.

That these concepts have paid off in terms of accomplishment over the past 75 years is evident from the number of repeat clients who have called upon the firm for solutions to their new problems and the number of major undertakings in which the firm has participated. Proceeding into the next quarter-century, the firm looks forward to a continuation of service to the construction industry in meeting new challenges in foundation engineering.

REFERENCES

The following references are made to the numbered footnotes in each chapter:

Chapter 1:

(1) Personal account (typescript) by Daniel Moran, page 4, describing his experiences with Charles Sooysmith.

(2) "Foundations Are More Art Than Science," *Engineering News-Record*, May 19, 1960.

(3) "Foundations that Will Endure," by Daniel E. Moran, *Harper's Weekly*, October 16, 1909.

(4) "Dan Moran, Foundation Builder," ENR News of the Week, *Engineering News-Record*, July 15, 1937.

(5) "Foundations," by Daniel E. Moran, *Engineers and Engineering*, February 1925.

(6) "Dan Moran, Foundation Builder," ENR News of the Week, *Engineering News-Record*, July 15, 1937.

(7) Obituary of Dan Moran, *Engineering News-Record*, July 15, 1937.

(8) Address before the Engineers Club, New York City, October 28, 1924.

(9) *Foundation Engineering*, Peck, Hanson, and Thornburn, New York, 1953.

(10) Obituary by F. E. Schmitt, editor of *Engineering News-Record*, July 15, 1937.

Chapter 2:

(1) "Golden Jubilee," paperback history, Construction Division, American Society of Civil Engineers, November 1975.

Chapter 3:

(1) "11,000 Tons on Wheels," by William H. Mueser, *The Technology Review*, July 1931.

(2) "Rigid Rectangular Frame Foundation for Albany Telephone Building," *Engineering News-Record*, November 27, 1930.

(3) "Ignoring Precedent in Rearing a Giant Skyscraper," by Carlton S. Proctor, *Real Estate Magazine*, August 1930.

Chapter 4:

(1) "Foundations," *Transactions of the American Society of Civil Engineers*, Centennial issue, Vol. CI, 1953.

(2) "The Main Piers of the Bridge over the Delaware River, Between Philadelphia and Camden," by Clement E. Chase, presented at the meeting of the Franklin Institute, February 21, 1923.

(3) "Pneumatic Caissons Sunk 110 Ft. for Vicksburg Bridge," by R. G. Stowell, *Engineering News-Record*, September 12, 1929.

(4) "Deep Cofferdam for Hudson River Bridge," by R.L. Telford, *Engineering News-Record*, August 16, 1928.

(5) "Building Pier 13 — The Deepest Substructure of the Suisun Bay Bridge," by C.R. Harding, *Contractors and Engineers Monthly*, July 1930.

(6) "Pier Foundations for the New Orleans Bridge," by N.F. Helmers, *Civil Engineering*, July 1936.

(7) "Settlement Studies of Huey P. Long Bridge," by William P. Kimball, *Civil Engineering*, March 1940.

Chapter 5:

(1) "A Practicing Engineer Looks at Soil Mechanics," by George L. Freeman, *Civil Engineering*, December 1938.

(2) "Review of Uses of Vertical Sand Drains," by Philip C. Rutledge and Stanley C. Johnston. Presented at the 36th Annual Meeting of the Highway Research Board, Washington, D.C., January 1957.

Chapter 6:

(1) "Apollo — A Trip to the Moon," a three-part report by the editors, *Civil Engineering*, ASCE, January 1965.

Chapter 8:

(1) "Underpinning Austin Dam," George L. Freeman and Robert B. Alsop, *Engineering News-Record*, January 30, 1941.

Chapter 9:

(1) Address by Daniel E. Moran before the Engineers Club, New York City, October 1922.

(2) "Recent Developments in Foundation Design," by Carlton S. Proctor, *Journal of the American Concrete Institute*, May-June 1937.

(3) "Utilization of Marginal Lands for Urban Development," by Philip C. Rutledge, *Journal of the Soil Mechanics and Foundations Division*, ASCE, January 1970.

(4), (5) "Landfill vs. Pile Platforms," address by Robert C. Johnston before the ASCE Annual National Engineering Meeting, October 30, 1973.

Chapter 11:

(1) "Graphical Representation of the Mechanical Analyses of Soils," by Frank B. Campbell. Discussion by Carlton S. Proctor, *ASCE Transactions*, 1939, Volume 104.

(2) "Survey of Causes of Settlement and Limitations of Analyses," by Philip C. Rutledge, discussion before the Metropolitan Section of the ASCE, April 9, 1973.

MORAN'S PATENTS

DATE	NUMBER	TITLE	CO-PATENTEE
June 27, 1893	500,149	Air-lock	
Dec. 3, 1895	550,798	Sand-drier	
Mar. 9, 1897	578,495	Derrick	
Apr. 10, 1900	647,274	Pin or Bolt Driving Hammer	
Dec. 17, 1901	689,109	Bolt Connection for Grinding Plates	
Mar. 11, 1902	694,978	Air-lock	
Apr. 21, 1903	725,751	Caisson or Cofferdam	E.S. Jarrett assignors, 1/3 to F. Remington
May 10, 1904	759,388	Caisson	Assignor of 2/3 to E.S. Jarrett & F. Remington
May 10, 1904	759,389	Caisson	Assignor of 2/3 to E.S. Jarrett & F. Remington
Feb. 14, 1905	782,410	Cofferdam	J.W. Doty
Aug. 14, 1906	828,761	Caisson	J.W. Doty
Aug. 14, 1906	828,861	Shafting for Caissons and the Like	J.W. Doty
Sept. 11, 1906	830,515	Construction and Sinking of Caissons, etc.	
Sept. 11, 1906	830,516	Construction and Sinking of Caissons, etc.	
Oct. 23, 1906	823,791	Construction and Sinking of Caissons, etc.	
Oct. 23, 1906	823,792	Construction and Sinking of Caissons, etc.	
July 2, 1907	858,742	Pile and Forming and Sinking It	
Aug. 27, 1907	864,383	Means for Resisting Lateral Hydraulic Pressures on Power-houses and Similar Structures	J.W. Doty
June 8, 1909	923,984	Sinking Shafts and the Like	
June 8, 1909	923,985	Dam and Building the Same	J.W. Doty and E.S. Jarrett
Sept. 14, 1909	933,776	Sinking Shafts and the Like	J.W. Doty and E.S. Jarrett
June 21, 1910	961,788	Sinking Shafts or the Like	
Aug. 27, 1912	1,036,680	Building Piers, Shafts, etc.	
Aug. 27, 1912	1,036,681	Sinking Joint-Caissons and Building Piers, Walls, etc.	
Sept. 26, 1916	1,199,485	Ventilating Tunnels	
Oct. 25, 1921	1,394,571	Subaqueous Structures and Methods	
Aug. 31, 1926	1,598,300	Foundations and the Like	
May 9, 1933	1,907,854	Sinking Foundations	
May 15, 1934	1,958,487	The Storage of Gasoline and the Like	
Aug. 21, 1934	1,971,046	Sinking Piers, Caissons, and the Like	
Nov. 12, 1935	2,021,014	Sinking Cellular Piers and the Like	
CANADA			
Dec. 24, 1935	354,884	Sinking Piers, Caissons, and the Like	
PORTUGAL			
Jan. 11, 1935	1079 de Classe 12^a	"Pilares imersos, caioes para funda coes e semelhones" (Sinking Piers, Caissons, and the Like)	